A man comes across an ancient enemy, beaten and left for dead. He lifts the wounded man onto the back of a donkey and takes him to an inn to tend to the man's recovery. Jesus tells this story and instructs those who are listening to "go and do likewise."

Likewise books explore a compassionate, active faith lived out in real time. When we're skeptical about the status quo, Likewise books challenge us to create culture responsibly. When we're confused about who we are and what we're supposed to be doing, Likewise books help us listen for God's voice. When we're discouraged by the troubled world we've inherited, Likewise books encourage us to hold onto hope.

In this life we will face challenges that demand our response. Likewise books face those challenges with us so we can act on faith.

LIKEWISE.   *Go and do.*

likewisebooks.com

GETTING YOUR FEET DIRTY

A Down-to-Earth Look at Following Jesus

Don Everts

IVP Books

An imprint of InterVarsity Press
Downers Grove, Illinois

InterVarsity Press
P.O. Box 1400, Downers Grove, IL 60515-1426
World Wide Web: www.ivpress.com
E-mail: email@ivpress.com

InterVarsity Press® is the book-publishing division of InterVarsity Christian
Fellowship/USA®, a student movement active on campus at hundreds of
universities, colleges and schools of nursing in the United States of America,
and a member movement of the International Fellowship of Evangelical Students.
For information about local and regional activities, write Public Relations Dept.,
InterVarsity Christian Fellowship/USA, 6400 Schroeder Rd., P.O. Box 7895,
Madison, WI 53707-7895, or visit the IVCF website at <www.intervarsity.org>.

Scripture quotations are taken from the Holy Bible, Today's New International
Version® TNIV® Copyright © 2001, 2005 by International Bible Society®. All
rights reserved worldwide.

Design: Cindy Kiple
Images: Brian Bailey/Getty Images

ISBN 978-0-8308-3604-8

Printed in the United States of America ∞

Library of Congress Cataloging-in-Publication Data

Everts, Don, 1971-
  Getting your feet dirty: a down-to-earth look at following Jesus/
Don Everts.
    p. cm.
  Includes bibliographical references.
  ISBN 978-0-8308-3604-8 (pbk.: alk. paper)
  1. Conversion—Christianity. 2. Christian life. 3.
  Conversion—Biblical teaching. 4. Christian life—Biblical teaching.
  5. Bible. N.T. Acts II—Criticism, interpretation, etc. I. Title.
  BV4921.3.E94 2007
  248.2'4—dc22

                                                            2006101566

P 17 16 15 14 13 12 11 10 9 8 7 6 5 4 3 2 1
Y 20 19 18 17 16 15 14 13 12 11 10 09 08 07

CONTENTS

WELCOME TO THE DELIVERY ROOM

(an introduction)

It was a Friday night I'll never forget.

My wife and I had gone out to a wonderful, extended dinner with friends. We came back to our apartment, watched an inconsequential movie and fell blissfully asleep. And that's when my wife started screaming.

You should know that she was pregnant. Quite pregnant. And that we were first-time parents, clueless and ecstatic. So when my wife started screaming, writhing in pain on the bed and cussing like a sailor, I assumed that must be normal.

I assumed every new father had to call 911 with one hand while trying to mop up a strange liquid with the other, all the while trying to calm this strange woman before him with brilliant commentary like "I'm sure this is just the beginning of contractions, honey. Are you remembering to breathe?"

I started to realize things weren't normal when I heard the 911 operator say, "Sir, have you ever delivered a baby before?"

Pause. "Excuse me," I said. "Have I ever delivered a baby before?"

Like I said, it was a Friday night I'll never forget.

But don't worry too much. This wasn't the beginning of a tragedy—a comedy maybe. Whatever it was, it was rated R, that's for sure. It was the beginning of a birth. Our firstborn, Simon, was beginning to make his way into our world. And just like many births, his entrance into this world was sloppy, hilarious, excruciating and elegant. That's what getting born is like.

About twenty exhausting hours after my wife started screaming, I found myself staring at an unbelievably tiny human being. My mind was full of images from the last twenty hours: the bright interior of the ambulance, the foreign world of the delivery room, the elegantly fierce looks on my wife's face, the sight of long needles and complex tubes and calm nurses and . . . and more bodily fluids than I want to describe here. With all these images swirling through my head, I stood there staring down at this tiny thing, just gaping at the marvel of it all.

I had witnessed the absolute wonder of birth.

BEING BORN ANEW

But what does that Friday night have to do with Jesus? Well, you see, one time a guy named Nicodemus walked up to Jesus (John 3). Nicodemus was a ruler of the Jews, an influential guy. But even though he wore a long robe and had a huge beard, he was really like many of us: intrigued by Jesus and wanting to know more.

Perhaps Nicodemus had recognized Jesus' revolutionary posture, had heard his countercultural teachings and had seen his tender embrace of the poor and marginalized. Whatever it was, Nicodemus couldn't help but stare at Jesus, just like many of us would do. And Nicodemus also couldn't help but wonder, just like many of us do, what it would be like to be one of his followers. To give up everything and get our own feet dirty, following this exquisite man.

And so Nicodemus walked up to Jesus with all his unspoken questions swirling through his head: *What do you really stand for, Jesus? Are you God? If someone wanted to follow you, what would they do? And what will happen to me if I do start following you? And are you really worth giving up everything to follow? And if I do, will my feet get as dirty as yours?*

Nicodemus brought all his questions to Jesus at night (probably not wanting to be found out by his peers) and started to talk with him. But early in the conversation Jesus looked right in his eyes and said, "Nicodemus, no one can see my kingdom unless they are born anew."

Born anew? Nicodemus was confused. Was Jesus joking? Was this another one of his parables? Nicodemus looked back into Jesus' eyes and asked, "But how can a full grown man be born all over again? Is he supposed to enter his mother's womb a second time?"

Jesus clarified. "You must be born of the Spirit. That which is born of the flesh is flesh. You need to be born of the Spirit, Nicodemus." And thus Jesus welcomed Nicodemus to be born all over again, as a follower of his.

Being born "of the flesh" I know something about. I distinctly remember that Friday night when my wife started screaming. And based on Simon's birth, I can safely say that being born of the flesh is *a wonder*. It's scary and confusing and exhilarating and serious and mysterious. And, in the end, an absolute marvel.

But what is it like to be born of the Spirit? What exactly was Jesus talking to Nicodemus about? What is it like to be born anew as a follower of Jesus? Is it just an emotional thing? Does this rebirth have to involve responding to an altar call at a church service or being baptized in a river or hearing a voice from heaven? Is it messy? Will I have to pretend I don't have any more questions?

Great questions, all of them very much worth asking.

In order to find some clear answers to these questions, I propose we watch some folks being born anew as followers of Jesus. After all, the birthing class my wife and I took was nice, but it was nothing compared to being in the real delivery room itself, watching Wendy push and seeing Simon come out. The theoretical stuff from the class I have forgotten almost all of. What happened in that delivery room is unforgettable.

THREE THOUSAND NEW BABIES

I propose we travel back in time—almost two thousand years back. The scene is Jerusalem. The event is what you might consider the first Christian church service ever. On that day something happened to three thousand people: they were born of the Spirit.

If you want to seriously consider what it's like to become a follower of Jesus, I can think of no better vantage point for you than the detailed descriptions of what happened on that day. This little book you are holding is a sustained, careful look at what did happen that day.

The events of that day are recorded in the second chapter of a biblical book called the Acts of the Apostles. And in that chapter (Acts 2) we have a front-row seat to some amazing action: people will become Jesus followers before our very eyes, being born of the Spirit.

And while the story of those three thousand people is their story and not ours, it is a story worth watching. We can hold the events of that day in our hands for a time and stare unabashedly and ask questions without reservation. In the end we can walk away from the "delivery room" with a much clearer understanding of what becoming a Christian is really all about.

In the first part of the book—"The Wonder of Birth"—we'll take a look at how those three thousand people went from being like everyone else in the crowd to being brand-new followers of Jesus. Watching their birthing process can be very helpful for those of us who are attracted to Jesus but don't know what it means to become one of his followers. If you have questions about the rebirth process, these first four chapters might be of particular interest to you.

In the second part—"The Joy of Being Alive"—we'll look at what their lives looked like *after* they were born of the Spirit. These three thousand people started living differently, and it is interesting to see what life was like for them after they became followers of Jesus. These last four chapters should be helpful for those of us who are still just curious and also for those of us who have become Christians and want to know what's in store for us.*

And right at the end there's a short section for Christian folks who might be reading this book to get better prepared to help out in the delivery room from time to time. If you are one of these folks, it might be helpful to check out this last section ("What About Us?") before starting in on the main two parts of the book.

We'll walk through both of these parts pretty slowly,

---

*In both parts we'll be looking at the ancient record of what happened that day. This record is nearly twenty centuries old, but it has been painstakingly preserved throughout the years and, relatively recently, translated into modern English. You can find a copy of this record, called the Acts of the Apostles, in any copy of the New Testament of the Bible. I've recorded references to, and quotes from, the Bible in standard notation: book, chapter, verse. For example, Acts 2:1-3 indicates a reference to the book of Acts, the second chapter, verses 1 through 3. John 3 is a reference to the book of John, the entire third chapter.

stopping along the way to ask questions and notice details and think about our own lives. By the end I hope we'll all have a clearer picture of what it means to get our feet dirty following this Jesus.

But enough lingering in the waiting room. Let's all wash up, put on our hospital gowns and step into the wonderful mess of the delivery room.

the wonder of birth

Jesus said the way to start following him was to be born of the Spirit.

But how exactly did his earliest followers get born like that?

And what would that look like today?

THE ACTION

what happened back then?

The story of the first three thousand people to become followers of Jesus and join his church is a story about a real thing. It really did happen. And it happened to real, historical people. Something happened to those three thousand people there in Jerusalem, something that we can read about and consider and weigh and ask questions about.

We need to be clear, though, that this overview of the events of that day isn't helpful because it is a detailed description of what it looks like *every single time* someone is born anew as a Christian. It is helpful because it gives us a detailed case study. And a case study gives us a solid place to start.

We can watch these people as they are born of the Spirit, and we can learn a lot about what it means to become one of Jesus' followers. This case study can give us some handles and language for understanding the process of spiritual birth that Jesus told Nicodemus about. And with these handles and this language, we can better ask the questions within us.

We'll read their story slowly and carefully. We'll look in detail at what happened that day. And we'll try to find out what was normative about their experience (important for every conversion) and what was unique about it (how subsequent conversions have looked different and will continue to look different).

We'll also look at what Jesus himself taught about becoming one of his followers and how that further illuminates these events in Acts 2.

But before getting into all the details like that, we need a fly-by. We need to hear the whole story of what happened that day, from beginning to end.

ACT I: THE NOISE

Once upon a time there was a bunch of Jesus followers. They were a ragtag group in some ways, mostly blue-collar workers and poor folks. Peter, Andrew, James, Mary—they were all Jewish and wore typical Jewish garb. The men wore long beards and everyone was in robes. They spoke to each other in Aramaic, many with rural accents.

This group was staying together in a city called Jerusalem, and on this day they were making a lot of noise. I mean, *a lot* of noise. They were speaking about God and how great he was and about everything he had done through Jesus. But they were quite loud about it all and were (seemingly miraculously) speaking in all sorts of foreign languages that none of them had ever studied or spoken before.

Not surprisingly a crowd began to form.

People staying all over the city heard the great noise and came to see what was the matter and who could be making such a noise. This crowd was huge and was made up of Jewish pilgrims staying in Jerusalem for one of their important festivals. Coming from countries all over the known world, they had each crossed many miles and many cultural barriers to make it to Jerusalem. Miriam, Stephen, Nicanor, Silas, Timon, Hannah, Abram—thousands of them gathered around this small group of local Jews.

Miriam turned to her husband, Azariah, and asked him the same question that was coming from everyone else in the crowd: "What's all the noise about?"

Azariah just shrugged and stared.

The crowd grew and grew, and eventually Nicanor, Abram and the others in the crowd began turning to each other with quizzical looks on their faces. "What's going on here? How is it that these people are speaking in so many different languages? Aren't they all simple Galileans? Do you hear them speaking in your native tongue too? So why are they talking about God like this?"

Everyone in the crowd was perplexed and amazed.

But the perplexed looks on some people's faces

turned into sneers. Abram shook his head and turned to his sister Hannah: "Listen to them, Hannah, these people must be drunk! Look at them, they are completely wasted! Silas, do you hear their drunken songs?" And so some people started making fun of the Jesus followers. Hannah laughed at them. Silas and his teenage friends started yelling out taunts and mimicking their talk.

But many others in the crowd still had perplexed looks on their faces, not sneers. They were genuinely con-fused. They had never seen anything like this nor heard any noise like this. So they began to ask a new question.

ACT II: THE STORY

Azariah looked back at his wife, Miriam, with wide eyes. "Miriam, what does all this mean?" This new question went beyond the specifics of the noise (How can they speak in my language?) to a deeper level (What is the meaning of all this?).

Eventually Peter, one of the leaders of the ragtag group, stood up and raised his voice so that all in the crowd could hear his answer to their question.

Looking toward Silas and his friends, he said, "Listen, I know what it looks like; I understand why you've jumped to the conclusion that everyone here must be drunk. But we're not. That's not what's going on here at all. It's only nine in the morning, after all!"

The crowd murmured a bit and then Peter told them

what was really going on. He told them the whole story. The whole Jesus story, that is. The Jesus story explained to everyone just what was going on with this ragtag group of Jesus followers and why they were speaking so loudly about God in foreign languages.

This story about Jesus was at once ancient (involving long-dead prophets and kings who were dear to everyone in the crowd) and also immediate (involving events many of them had seen take place in Jerusalem). The story was both mysterious (melding history, spirituality, God, men and women, joy, eternity, death, current events, murder, ancient prophecy) and also very clear (the story was not overly long or obtuse or in some code language).

When Peter had finished telling the story, the people in the crowd were cut to the heart. Cut. To the heart.

The story had gone directly into the deepest parts of them. Silas wasn't joking anymore, and some of his friends stared at the ground thoughtfully. Miriam glanced at her husband and they exchanged a knowing look. Abram stroked his long, full beard. Many in the crowd had become involved in the story and it had cut them to their hearts. They leaned toward Peter and the other followers of Jesus because they had another question to ask.

ACT III: THE CALL

Abram looked around at those near him, a few tears glistening in his rough beard. Eventually he loudly spoke the question that was rising from many of their hearts: "Peter, brothers, what then should we do?"

And Peter answered Abram's question. He told him (and everyone who looked at him with that same look) what they should do.

Looking into the eyes of Abram, into the eyes of those around him, Peter said, "Repent and be baptized, every one of you. Do this in the name of Jesus the Messiah, whose story you now know. And do it for the forgiveness of your sins. And then you will receive the gift of the Holy Spirit."

Peter looked out at the men and women who stood silent in their robes and continued, "This promise is for you. For all of you and for your children. And even for people who are far away from Jerusalem! This promise is for everyone God calls to him."

And Peter wasn't through yet. With many other words, he warned Silas and his friends and others in the crowd. He pleaded with them, trying to help them see the utter importance of the story and the crucial nature of responding to the story. "Save yourselves from this corrupt generation," he said.

And all those who accepted his message did repent and were baptized. About three thousand people became Jesus followers that day.

ACT IV: THE LIFE

After Hannah and Silas and Abram and about three thousand more had repented and been baptized, they had a final question rising in their hearts: *What happens next?*

And what came next was that these new followers of Jesus were his. They were reborn into the kingdom of God, and with Jesus as their King, everything began to change. They became people of devotion. They devoted themselves to the teachings of the original Jesus followers who had been with Jesus. They devoted themselves to each other. They devoted themselves to breaking bread with each other, as Jesus had taught his earliest followers to do. And they devoted themselves to talking with God and listening to God.

Their friends and neighbors were shocked at their devotion. Sure, Silas was still Silas, and Hannah was still Hannah, but something had happened to them. They were different now, obviously different. They were starting to look more like Jesus, their feet just as dirty as his.

And Abram and Nicanor and Sara and Silas and the rest of these new Jesus followers lived happily, joyfully, painfully, surprisingly, deeply, eternally . . . ever after.

The end.

WHAT YOU DO WITH A CASE STUDY

Well, the beginning, really. Ever since that day, people have continued to be perplexed at Jesus' followers, have continued to ask what the meaning of it all is, have continued to hear the Jesus story and be cut to the heart,

and have continued to repent and be baptized and believe in the story with all their lives.

And the Spirit of Jesus has continued to come into his
new followers. And they have continued to be people of
devotion. What sounded impossible to Nicodemus happened: they were born anew. And, as it turns out, new
followers of Jesus are born in every age.

Except it doesn't always happen three thousand people at a time. And the Jesus story isn't always told in Aramaic, to Jews. And sometimes the order is a little different. And . . .

Well, that's what the next few chapters are about:
looking more closely at what happened that first day and
asking our questions. What happened to Silas and Timon and Nicanor and Abram that day? And how does
this case study help us answer our own questions about
becoming followers of Jesus?

THE NOISE

are you guys drunk or what?

Our case study begins with a bang: the Spirit of God descends on a room, a ragtag group of Christians start speaking loudly in foreign languages and thousands of people gather around to see what in the world is going on.

When the day of Pentecost came, they were all together in one place. Suddenly a sound like the blowing of a violent wind came from heaven and filled the whole house where they were sitting. They saw what seemed to be tongues of fire that separated and came to rest on each of them. All of them were filled with the Holy Spirit and began to speak in other tongues as the Spirit enabled them.

Now there were staying in Jerusalem God-fearing Jews from every nation under heaven. When they heard this sound, a crowd came together in bewilderment, because each one heard their own language being spoken. Utterly amazed, they asked: "Aren't all these who are speaking Galileans? Then how is it that each of us hears them in our native language? Parthians, Medes and Elamites; residents of Meso-potamia, Judea and Cappadocia, Pontus and Asia, Phrygia and Pamphylia, Egypt and the parts of Libya near Cyrene; visitors from Rome (both Jews and con-verts to Judaism); Cretans and Arabs—we hear them declaring the wonders of God in our own tongues!" Amazed and perplexed, they asked one another, "What does this mean?"

Some, however, made fun of them and said, "They have had too much wine."

Then Peter stood up with the Eleven, raised his voice and addressed the crowd: "Fellow Jews and all of you who live in Jerusalem, let me explain this to you; listen carefully to what I say. These people are not drunk, as you suppose. It's only nine in the morning!" (Acts 2:1-15)

Quite a beginning to our case study, huh? Now, as spectacular as these events were, we need to realize that they weren't necessarily a surprise for Jesus' follow-ers. After all, Jesus had told them that he would send his Spirit to them (for example, John 14:15-21) and that they should wait in Jerusalem until the Spirit came (Acts 1:4). And he had also assured them that when the Spirit came into them they would receive power and this power would enable them to talk about Jesus to every nation (Acts 1:8).

But you've gotta know that the crowds in Jerusalem were most definitely surprised! All of a sudden these followers of Jesus were speaking in other languages even though they were all simple Galileans. What do you do with such a spectacle? How do you make sense of it? What in the world is going on in Jerusalem?

QUESTIONS ARE INEVITABLE

Wherever there are followers of Jesus, they seem to be making some kind of ruckus. They speak in foreign languages, they sing "Kumbaya" and strum guitars, they read Old English from the Bible, they invite their neighbors to come to church with them. Sometimes this leaves the people around them staring and scratching their heads in wonder.

I remember the first time I saw some Christians raising their hands during a church service. I stared. And I scratched my head in wonder. Why were they all holding their hands in the air?

But it's almost always like that with followers of Jesus—they often arouse questions from those around them. Our case study has some unique features (Christians aren't always speaking in other languages; the crowd isn't always so large or so Jewish or so multinational), but one thing has remained true ever since that day—Jesus followers are conspicuous and so questions about them are inevitable.

Jesus was clear from the beginning that his followers would be upside down from the rest of the world and would stick out in a crowd. After describing what his followers would come to look like over time, he told them explicitly, "You are the light of the world. A city on a hill cannot be hidden. Neither do people light a lamp and put it under a bowl. Instead they put it on its stand, and it gives light to everyone in the house. In the same way, let your light shine before others, that they may see your good deeds and glorify your Father in heaven" (Matthew 5:14-16).

Jesus also likened his followers to salt—something that sticks out and is noticed by its taste. Now, Jesus was definitely saying something about the *effect* Jesus followers would have in the world (light illumines, salt preserves), but he was also clear that they would stick out and be conspicuous. They would be noticed. They would no longer fit in like everyone else.

I've experienced this myself. Having a King, and having the Spirit of Jesus inside me, has slowly begun to affect my view of this world around me and my participation with it. I take my family and groups of college students to live in the inner city of Denver on a regular basis; I have traveled to the slums of a megacity to learn from the people there; my wife and I try to live a simple lifestyle in the midst of an affluent suburban community; I'm not so concerned about protecting my rights; I forgive . . . And all that gets noticed. It makes me stick out.

After returning from Denver one summer, I stood at my back fence talking with my next-door neighbor (a college professor), who thought it odd that I had taken my pregnant wife and one-year-old, Simon, to live in Sun Valley (one of the poorest, most dangerous neighborhoods in Denver). He had lots of questions to ask me about this and a perplexed look on his face as he listened to my answers. I had gotten my feet dirty with Jesus and it made me conspicuous.

I have a friend, Tenille, who mourns for the pains of the world. Tenille's not depressed and she's not ambivalent (two postures that are common in her town). Instead she mourns. She sees the brokenness and hardships of the world, and they make her mourn. She cries often in prayer and feels deeply what she sees. I've even seen tears flow from her eyes as she stood in line at a McDonald's witnessing blatant racism between a customer and an employee.

It's not that she has always been this way. But once Tenille became a Christian, God started changing her heart into a heart that mourns for the pains of the world. And in the calm, entertainment-engorged, polite town she lives in, her mourning draws some strange looks.

But Jesus said it would be so. To be one of his would

mean we stick out and are conspicuous. Followers of Jesus make people turn and take notice. That was the case that day in Jerusalem, and it always is.

QUESTIONS ARE GOOD

Because Jesus followers stick out so much, it only makes sense that people will try to make sense of what they see in them. Asking questions about these odd Christians is just natural. The questions are real, so it's a good thing to ask them.

Jerusalem was not a city where people magically began speaking in other languages, so it was natural for Abram and Hannah and Silas to ask some questions when these Christians immediately start speaking other languages.

Today, in countries where tolerance and do-it-yourself spirituality are assumed, it's natural to ask questions when you meet Jesus followers who insist that there can be only one truth—and that they've found it. In an age when sin is seen as an archaic, naive concept, it makes sense that people would have questions about Jesus followers who speak of sin often (and with straight faces!).

Sometimes the questions are highly emotional. Sometimes they are intellectual. I had one friend, Matthew, who was intrigued by Jesus but was so used to hating Christians that he couldn't imagine becoming one of them. So he asked all sorts of questions about why

Jesus followers do what they do: "Why do Christians wear T-shirts that proclaim their faith? Why do Christians pray with accents and vocabulary that they never use when talking with me? Why do they make such a big deal of sin and judgment?"

Matthew's questions made sense to me. But not only did his questions make sense; I think they were good. And important. Jesus had the highest praise for people who stuck around to ask him questions (Mark 4:1-11) and the harshest reactions to those who were stubborn and silent and had no questions to ask (Mark 3:4-5). Jesus loved it when people asked the questions that were brewing inside them.

It was natural that Azariah and Miriam had questions that day in Jerusalem, and it was good that they asked them. And the same has been true ever since. Whenever someone becomes a Jesus follower, it seems that asking lots of questions comes somewhere in the process. It's an important part of being born anew as a follower of Jesus.

I know that for me there were certain questions I just *had* to ask about Jesus and his followers when I was considering following Jesus. "Why do they sing with their hands in the air? Why does the pastor wear a robe? Why are there so many different churches?" I found that I had to ask those questions, that there was no getting around them.

But I also found that I had to look somewhere other than my imagination to find some real answers.

QUESTIONS ARE NOT ANSWERS

Another thing we learn from that first day in Jerusalem is that questions don't always lead to answers when we try to answer them all by ourselves.

On that day in Jerusalem everyone in the crowd was asking each other, "How is this possible?" They were all standing and staring at the same thing. But none of them had been there when the Spirit had come upon the Jesus followers prior to their speaking in tongues. And no one in the crowd had been with Jesus weeks earlier when he promised the disciples that the Holy Spirit would come upon them. And yet the folks in that crowd (go back and read the description of that day) were asking *each other* what was going on. Azariah was asking his wife, Miriam. Tall Abram was asking his friends standing near him.

Now, in retrospect it may seem silly to expect anyone in the crowd to be able to answer the question. But, silly or not, there were many there who jumped right in and tried to answer the question themselves: "Well, they must be drunk!"

We know that isn't a very good answer. They hadn't been drinking. And even if they had, who has ever been able to intelligibly speak a foreign language they had never studied . . . all because they were drunk? I've never been drunk like that! It's a silly answer, isn't it? But when we try to answer our own questions by ourselves, we often come up with answers like that.

This has continued to happen throughout the centuries as crowds stare over at the Jesus followers making their Christian "noises" and try to explain it all away by themselves.

Why are Jesus followers so blindly clinging to the Bible? "Well, they must be brainwashed folks who aren't very literate." Why do they insist on trying to "share" their Christian religion with me? "They must be completely arrogant or ignorant—or both." Why do they insist on talking about Jesus all the time? "They must be pretty simplistic people, unable to open their minds to apprehend greater truths."

In college, when the guys in the dorm found out I wasn't sleeping with my girlfriend, they came up with their own explanations for this perplexing behavior: "He must be a prude. Or gay." (Neither of which was true.) When I began purposefully living a simple lifestyle, throwing away dozens of trophies from high school, giving away many of my clothes and possessions, many people close to me concluded, "Don is such an irresponsible slouch." (Nope.) And when my neighbor heard about my summer in Sun Valley, he nodded and commented, "You must be a really nice guy." (Unfortunately that's not right either.)

The answer to all their questions actually had much more to do with the fact that I had been born anew into Jesus' kingdom. But how could any of them have known that on their own?

Just like in our case study in Jerusalem, people who are perplexed by Jesus' followers don't necessarily go up and ask the Jesus followers themselves; they sit back and stare and wonder and hypothesize and come up with their own answers. Answers that are sometimes simply wrong.

WHAT ABOUT ME?

1. Ask the questions that you have.

What "noise" coming from Christians has caught your attention and has you perplexed? If you find yourself perplexed, feel free to ask the questions that are inside you.

For example, if you're wondering what Christians believe about the Bible, ask those questions honestly. If you're perplexed about how Jesus followers live and why they live that way, find somewhere to get answers to those questions. If you wonder why there are so many different kinds of churches, try to find out why. Remember, Jesus encouraged questions and was saddened when people sat on their questions and would no longer engage with him.

Whether you are a follower of Jesus or not, you likely

have some questions about Christians or Christianity. It would be dishonest to stuff the questions and move on. So ask your questions.

Having said that, let me add that you should be sure to ask your questions in good places. For example, you could try to answer your own questions, but as we've seen, that might not be the best strategy. Even talking with other perplexed people standing in the crowd with you might not be the best place to start. But there are a number of other resources available to you.

Peter isn't still around to field your questions, but there are plenty of Christians in your own neighborhood who could talk with you frankly about your questions. Pick a

You could also look for some books that address your questions. Do a search online. Or walk into a local Christian bookstore, and someone behind the counter will likely be able to point you toward helpful books. If your questions range all over, I'd suggest getting your hands on Cliff Knechtle's *Help Me Believe: Direct Answers to Real Questions* (InterVarsity Press, 2000) or C. S. Lewis's fantastic little book called *Mere Christianity* (HarperSanFrancisco, 2001).

local pastor or a Christian you know well and buy this person a cup of coffee. Then ask the Christian your questions and see what he or she says.

2. Ask the big question and listen to the whole story.

There was a shift that day when the crowds asked what the meaning beneath it all was. And that shift was important.

If they had continued to ask the specific questions ("How are Galileans able to speak our languages?"), they might never have gotten the real answers they wanted. By asking that specific question, which focused them in on the phenomenon of speaking in other languages, they were unknowingly forming the conversation around that one specific topic. They weren't asking about *what* was being said (the mighty acts of God being declared) or *why* it was all happening to so many people at the same time (spontaneous, loud worship is strange, no matter what language we're talking about!).

Though they could have gotten myopically stuck on that one issue, they didn't. Instead they eventually became so amazed and perplexed that they asked a general, sweeping question: "What does all this mean?" And they let Peter answer that sweeping question. And that shift in the crowd was what allowed them to get the answers they were looking for.

That continues to be the case today. Eventually you may also recognize that your questions are not necessarily going to lead you to understanding the entirety of what this Jesus follower thing is all about. Reading multiple books on creationism may be helpful for you in answering some of your specific questions, but the reality is, those books won't necessarily take you to the core of what's going on with all these Christians you know.

Just like Peter, Jesus' followers throughout the centuries always seem to pull back to the Jesus story, implying that it's never entirely about the creation story or the Crusades story or the why-there-are-so-many-different-kinds-of-churches story. And implying that no questions about his followers (whatever the noise of the day may be) can fully be answered without understanding that which is at the core of every one of his followers—Jesus himself.

After all, this phenomenon called Christianity is all about Jesus. And just as the crowd on that day in Jerusalem eventually allowed Peter to tell them his story, we each must get to a place where we recognize the limitations of our own questions and simply ask, "What does this mean?" and then allow a Jesus follower the time to tell us the whole story about Jesus.

can you just start over at the beginning?

Our case study now moves on to story time. Abram and Azariah and Hannah and the rest want to know the meaning of what they are seeing. And so Peter lets them in on the meaning by telling them a story. The Jesus story, that is.

Peter stood up with the Eleven, raised his voice and addressed the crowd: "Fellow Jews and all of you who live in Jerusalem, let me explain this to you; listen carefully to what I say. These people are not drunk, as you suppose. It's only nine in the morning! No, this is what was spoken by the prophet Joel:

"'In the last days, God says,
    I will pour out my Spirit on all people.
Your sons and daughters will prophesy,
    your young men will see visions,
    your old men will dream dreams.
Even on my servants, both men and women,
    I will pour out my Spirit in those days,

and they will prophesy.
I will show wonders in the heaven above
and signs on the earth below,
blood and fire and billows of smoke.
The sun will be turned to darkness
and the moon to blood
before the coming of the great and glorious
day of the Lord.
And everyone who calls
on the name of the Lord will be saved.'

"People of Israel, listen to this: Jesus of Nazareth was a man accredited by God to you by miracles, wonders and signs, which God did among you through him, as you yourselves know. This man was handed over to you by God's deliberate plan and foreknowledge; and you, with the help of wicked men, put him to death by nailing him to the cross. But God raised him from the dead, freeing him from the agony of death, because it was impossible for death to keep its hold on him. David said about him:

"'I saw the Lord always before me.
Because he is at my right hand,
I will not be shaken.
Therefore my heart is glad and my tongue rejoices;
my body also will rest in hope,

because you will not abandon me to the grave,
*   you will not let your holy one see decay.*
You have made known to me the paths of life;
*   you will fill me with joy in your presence.'*

"Brothers and sisters, we all know that the patriarch David died and was buried, and his tomb is here to this day. But he was a prophet and knew that God had promised him on oath that he would place one of his descendants on his throne. Seeing what was to come, he spoke of the resurrection of the Messiah, that he was not abandoned to the realm of the dead, nor did his body see decay. God has raised this Jesus to life, and we are all witnesses of the fact. Exalted to the right hand of God, he has received from the Father the promised Holy Spirit and has poured out what you now see and hear. For David did not ascend to heaven, and yet he said,

"'The Lord said to my Lord:
*   "Sit at my right hand*
until I make your enemies
*   a footstool for your feet."'*

"Therefore let all Israel be assured of this: God has made this Jesus, whom you crucified, both Lord and Messiah."

When the people heard this, they were cut to the heart and said to Peter and the other apostles, "Brothers, what shall we do?" (Acts 2:14-37)

That's quite a story Peter told that day. The people wanted to know the meaning of all they had witnessed and heard, so Peter told them.

Now, there's plenty about Peter's telling of the story that is unique to our case study. It was Peter telling the story. And he was speaking to a specific crowd. But while the telling of the Jesus story has obviously varied in style and length and language and posture since that first telling, there's still plenty we can learn from Peter's words that day.

THE JESUS STORY IS HISTORIC

The first thing we learn is that the meaning behind what was happening was a person, Jesus. Sure, Peter began by noting that they weren't drunk (dispelling one of the rumors that had begun floating around the crowd), but then he went on to spend most of his time talking about a person. He told Hannah and Abram and Silas the Jesus story.

And the Jesus story (I imagine this should go without saying, but it *is* a significant point) is about Jesus. A person. A person who lived and taught and was killed and was seen again after his death and sent his Spirit into his followers, who then began praising God with loud voices. Jesus, ultimately, was the meaning behind what was going on that day. Rather than talking about ideas or philosophies or theories, Peter talks about a person—Jesus.

And Peter knows what he's talking about. Peter had met Jesus, after all. Peter had followed him for three eventful years, doing everything together. Peter saw everything Jesus did, heard all his teachings, saw what happened to him when he died . . . and then saw him alive again after three days. And it's those historic events and what they reveal about Jesus that Peter talks about that day.

It turns out that's all Peter kept talking about for the rest of his life. In one of Peter's letters that we still have today he writes, "We did not follow cleverly devised stories when we told you about the coming of our Lord Jesus Christ in power, but we were eyewitnesses of his majesty" (2 Peter 1:16). Peter always made sure that people knew he was talking about real historical happenings when he talked about Jesus.

And whenever that same story of Jesus has been told throughout the centuries, it's this historic nature of the story that always seems most important: the clear story of who Jesus was, what he did, what he taught and what happened during those fateful days in Jerusalem when he was hung on a cross and died . . . and then came back to life three days later.

Silas and his friends had likely heard many clichés and stereotypes about Jesus already. (Take your pick: he was a dangerous Jewish teacher; he was a drunkard; he was a political revolutionary set against Rome.) And yet it was hearing the story from Peter that day that changed them forever. It was as if they were hearing about the real Jesus for the first time. And it cut them to the heart.

That's more or less how it has continued to happen throughout the years. People are cut to the heart. Sometimes those who have never heard about Jesus (or have only heard cliché phrases about him) are affected deeply when they first hear the story.

My friend Matthew grew up in a Christian-saturated culture and had rejected out of hand this Christianity thing and the Christians he kept bumping into. He hated Christians and their silly T-shirts and arrogant messages and glaring hypocrisy. But one day when we were hanging out and he was eviscerating "those Christians everywhere," I asked him if he'd ever heard much about Jesus himself. He thought about it and realized he hadn't.

So I encouraged him to read some of the Gospel stories. He did. And he really liked Jesus. In fact, Matthew found him provocative and witty and . . . *strangely honest.* And so he read more. He gulped down the Gospel stories and found himself cut to the heart by this man and his message and his hanging on the cross. It wasn't Christianity that impressed Matthew; it was the simple stories about Jesus that had such an impact on him.

THE JESUS STORY IS TOLD TO PEOPLE

The second thing to notice about this story time in our case study is that Peter tells the story in a certain way.

For example, most of Peter's words are actually quotes from the Old Testament. Three times Peter quotes directly from the Hebrew Scriptures, which everyone in that thoroughly Jewish crowd would have been very familiar with. Peter speaks the cultural language of Abram and Hannah.

Peter's Jewish way of telling the story that day clarifies an important truth: while the content of the story (the person, Jesus) is set and never changes, the *form* of the story has varied widely throughout the centuries.

Peter uses a certain language, style and posture in his telling of the story. This is because Peter is telling the story *to people.* He is not speaking in a vacuum; he is speaking into human ears. And because Peter is speaking into Jewish ears, his tongue speaks in a Jewish way. And from then on, whenever the story is told best, it is told in a way people's ears can hear it.

Consider an early leader of the church, Paul. When Paul is telling the Jesus story in a synagogue in Pisidian Antioch, he is speaking to Jews. Read his telling of the story that day (Acts 13:16-41) and you'll see that his telling of the story is much like Peter's. But only days later, when Paul is in Lystra, he is speaking to Gentile people (non-Jews) who have various gods to whom they attribute all natural phenomena. Read his telling of the Jesus story that day (Acts 14:14-18) and you won't see a single quote from Hebrew Scriptures, but you will see Paul speaking of heaven and earth and sea and rain and crops—stuff they understand and think about. A bit later, when Paul is in urbane, sophisticated Athens, his telling of the story quotes from modern philosophers and local urban landmarks (Acts 17:22-31).

But why is this? Why doesn't Paul just have one way of telling the story of Jesus and repeat it the same way to everyone? Well, because Paul is telling the story *to people.* He contextualizes the story for those he is speaking to. And this contextualizing is an act of service. An act of service that shouldn't surprise us.

It shouldn't surprise us, because Jesus himself was the word that became flesh (John 1:14). God had a message of ultimate truth (the word), but God didn't want to just get out a megaphone and impersonally broadcast this message over the earth. Instead God chose to embody this message in a person, Jesus (the flesh). And Jesus came, as we're told, to dwell (literally, "pitch a tent") among the people (John 1:14).

The fact that Jesus came into a specific culture with a definite skin color and accent and *there* lived out his story should tell us something about God's respect and love for people. This is God's heart—to incarnate himself, to be near people. The Jesus story, then, isn't etched in stone somewhere. It is spoken into people's ears. In their very own heart language.

I grew up going to church every Sunday. Stained glass, organ, hymnals—the whole bit. Now, the story of me going to church is a long one, but one small part of that story is the simple fact that I could not hear what was being said in church. I just couldn't hear it. There I was every single week, sitting in a pew, listening intently (yes, *intently*), and I couldn't hear inside of me the story of Jesus that was being told there. Even though it was in English. I comprehended very little and was definitely never cut to the heart.

Fast-forward a bit and I am a skinny high school student standing on the deck of a large boat heading northward into the painfully beautiful Princess Louisa Inlet of British Columbia. And there, at Young Life's Malibu Camp, I heard the Jesus story for the first time. As the story was told simply through skits, through young speakers and in a language and vernacular that was easy to understand, I heard the Jesus story as if I had never even heard about Jesus before. And was cut. To the heart.

Today, just as on that day there in Jerusalem, the story of Jesus is meant to be heard by people. In their own language.

THE JESUS STORY IS SHARP AND PRESSING

It is also important to stop and consider the response
that Abram and Hannah and the rest had to the story. It's
important because their response shows us something
about the story itself. On that day after Peter told the
story, the crowd was not intrigued or interested; they
were cut to the heart.

The word for "cut" used in the original text literally
means "to stab thoroughly." There was something about
hearing the story about Jesus that stabbed into tough
Abram's heart, that pierced him inside.

I've had times in my life when a piece of news immediately affected my heart (finding out my brother was in
jail) or stirred emotions within me (hearing her whisper, "I
love you too"). I imagine that's something of what it was
like for Abram and the rest that day. It wasn't just emotional; it wasn't purely physical; it wasn't simply intellectual. It had stirred something soul-deep within them.

Jesus had always emphasized the heart, regularly dis-
missing people's surface responses and seeming much
more interested in what was going on *within* them. He likened his own teachings to "seeds" that were being
planted in the "soil" of people's hearts (see Mark 4:1-34).
He was never interested in adorning people or reapplying
their lipstick and rouge. He was interested in planting his
truth within people so that it would affect them from the
inside out.

So it makes sense that the Jesus story should have this same kind of effect on people. Jesus did say that, when he sent his Spirit, this Spirit would convict people, cutting them to the heart (John 16:8). And within the story itself we also see some sharp words that have the potential to cut.

You see, the people *themselves* are in the story. Peter reminds the crowd that Jesus "was handed over to *you* by God's deliberate plan and foreknowledge; and *you,* with the help of wicked men, put him to death by nailing him to the cross" (Acts 2:23, emphasis added). Right there, when Peter is proclaiming the story of Jesus' death, he makes it perfectly (and painfully) clear that Abram, Hannah and the rest are responsible. They share in the guilt of innocent Jesus being put to death.

It's *their own hands* that were holding the hammers and driving in the nails. It's *their own mouths* that were spouting insults at him. And most significantly, it's *their very own sins* that caused him to die and for which he chose to die.

The Jesus story is pressing precisely because it is *our* story. The Jesus story is pressing because it involves the cross, which immediately brings each of our sins into the story. And that makes the story come to life unlike any other story.

In Acts 8 we read of an African who is casually riding along in a chariot reading a book. He encounters a leader of the early church, Philip, and invites him aboard the chariot and they begin discussing the book the Ethiopian had been reading. This discussion (because of the book he was reading) eventually gets around to the person of Jesus, and Philip tells the Ethiopian the Jesus story. And just like that, without a drum roll, without a temple nearby, just riding along in the chariot, the Ethiopian is cut by the story. He sees himself in the story, and so when they pass by some water, the Ethiopian asks without ceremony if he can please be baptized in that very water and become a follower of Jesus, receiving forgiveness for his sins.

That's how it goes. Whether it happens while reading a book, listening to a friend or sitting alone somewhere mulling over years of messages, when a person hears the story, it can come into their soul as something pressing and urgent.

As I was hearing the Jesus story for the first time up in British Columbia (even though I had been in church nearly all my life), my best friend, Todd, was also hearing the story. Todd had never been to church a day in his life. And Todd was a practical guy, a good guy. Not excitable, not overly emotional. An athletic, common-sense kind of guy. But when he heard the telling that week up in Canada, something happened. He became more quiet than usual. When I went looking for him so we could go water-skiing or play basketball, I often found him sitting alone, staring out at the deep-blue waters of the inlet.

Todd's heart had been stabbed thoroughly by the telling that week. Just like the hearts of Abram and Hannah and young Silas. Just like the Ethiopian's heart. Just like my friend Matthew's. And mine. The reality is, the Jesus story is a pressing, urgent, invasive story. It was that day in Jerusalem, and it still is today.

WHAT ABOUT ME?

1. Find a telling of the story that you can hear.

It's one thing to ask detailed questions about Christian "noise" (see chapter two); it is quite another to ask for the meaning beneath everything and to hear the Jesus story. To move from smaller questions ("How are these Galileans able to speak all our languages?") to the biggest of questions ("What is the meaning of all this?") is an important move.

If you find yourself asking this question, then be sure to ask it in places where you can hear the story of Jesus. Get alone with some Christian and ask him or her to tell you the story. Go to a Christian church and listen to their telling of the story. While there, you'll likely hear a sermon. But Christians are usually so preoccupied with this Jesus story (and rightly so) that even their music and dramas and videos often tell the Jesus story as well. For me, it was a visual drama, not just the spoken word, that allowed me to hear the Jesus story for the first time.

But whether you are talking with a Christian friend over lunch, reading a book about Jesus, attending a church or watching a movie, make sure it's the Jesus story you are getting. There are many great conversations you could have or books you could read or sermons you could hear about a number of topics (as we mentioned in the last chapter), but to get at the meaning behind it all, you will want *the story itself.* You don't want the creationism story or the Christian morality story or even the Christianity story. You want the Jesus story. The telling of him as a person: what he said and did and what happened to him in Jerusalem.

The surest way of getting that story would be to read one of the ancient, original tell-

Each of these four Gospels has the same content (the person of Jesus) but has a different form, since each was written to a different group of people. Mark's the shortest, if you're looking for a quick read. John's the most poetic, artfully crafted telling. Luke was a physician, and his telling is very ordered. Matthew was writing to Jews, so there are all kinds of Old Testament references in his. The Gospels are all winners, though. You can't go wrong. If you read one of them, it's the Jesus story you'll hear.

ings of the story yourself. Matthew, Mark, Luke and John
are the four Gospels (literally, "tellings of the good news")
that you can find in any Bible, right there at the beginning
of the New Testament. Pick one and read through the
whole thing in one sitting. Hear the story from front to
back. There's nothing to help clear up our sometimes
stereotypical images of Jesus like reading one of the old-
est accounts of him.

2. Pay attention to your heart and soul.

If the Jesus story were a philosophical treatise, then you
could approach the story intellectually and dispassion-
ately—collect the data, analyze it, come to some conclu-
sions. If it were a story simply about how to live, you
could make a list and try some of it out and see how it
goes. But it's none of those things.

It's the story of a person. It's a historical story that is
pressing and important and that we find ourselves written into. And because of that, it is essential that as we listen to the story we pay attention to our hearts, our souls,
our intestines—the parts of us that are somehow con-
nected to the very core of our souls.

And if you do, either during the telling or sometime after the telling, find yourself stabbed in your heart, if you
are bothered, if the story about Jesus and what he did
and said and his hanging on that tree sticks into you like
a fishhook, then pay attention to that too. Note it. That

reaction may not be random or inconsequential. It might just mean something.

It could be that what is happening to you is much like what happened to those people that day in Jerusalem. And if that does happen, you may find yourself asking the very question that was next on the lips of the crowd that day: "Brothers, what then shall we do?"

THE CALL

where do I sign up?

In the last chapter we left our friends Abram, Hannah, Silas and the rest of the crowd cut to the heart. They were cut to the heart and asked Peter what they should do. They wanted to respond to the Jesus story; they just weren't sure how to. They knew they needed to do something; they just didn't know what. And so they asked what they should do. And Peter told them.

Peter replied, "Repent and be baptized, every one of you, in the name of Jesus Christ for the forgiveness of your sins. And you will receive the gift of the Holy Spirit. The promise is for you and your children and for all who are far off—for all whom the Lord our God will call."

With many other words he warned them; and he pleaded with them, "Save yourselves from this corrupt generation." Those who accepted his message were baptized, and about three thousand were added to their number that day. (Acts 2:38-41)

After Peter made clear what it was they should do in response to the story, Abram and Hannah and about three thousand more did exactly what he suggested. Three thousand men and women accepted his message and repented and were baptized. Yes, three thousand.

Now, that kind of response is unusual. That many people don't often respond to the call at the same time. And the message is not always accepted right away. But on that day they had an immediate response.

While the story of the three thousand is *their* story and not ours, it does clarify quite a bit for us. It is clarifying because there was nothing too special about how Peter answered their question about what they should do. He was simply echoing the words of Jesus. And since that day in Jerusalem, the core call of the church has been the same.

So Peter's answer to them that day is important for all of us today who want to know how to respond to Jesus and start getting our feet dirty following him too.

THE CALL WAS CLEAR

Peter was clear that day about what the people needed to do. "Repent and be baptized, every one of you," he said. Peter made it clear that they needed to repent. And that they needed to be baptized.

To repent is to change your mind (from the Greek *metanoia*). It means to turn around completely. To turn from your former life, your former worldview, your former set of assumptions, your former posture . . . and to turn toward Jesus and his gospel message. To repent is to turn and face the message of Jesus that you have heard and accept it. Repentance is a surrender of sorts. It is the act of kneeling at the feet of a King, Jesus, and giving your life to him.

From the beginning, Jesus' message was one of repentance. "Jesus went into Galilee, proclaiming the good news of God. 'The time has come,' he said. 'The kingdom of God has come near. Repent and believe the good news!' " (Mark 1:14-15).

This simple call was what he told his disciples (including Peter) to go and deliver as well. Speaking to them, Jesus said, "Go and make disciples of all nations, baptizing them in the name of the Father and of the Son and of the Holy Spirit, and teaching them to obey everything I have commanded you" (Matthew 28:19-20).

So Peter didn't make this up. It's what Jesus told him to say. He was to call people to repent and be baptized. And so he does. It is important to note that at this point of the day Peter does not tell the Jesus story again. He calls the people to specific actions. Peter, perhaps better than anyone, understood that there comes a time for action. For response. So there's not another story here; there's a call. And that is appropriate.

The next time Peter tells people about Jesus, we hear

the same call: "Repent, then, and turn to God, so that your sins may be wiped out, that times of refreshing may come from the Lord" (Acts 3:19). And that's always the call. Peter was just echoing the words of Jesus, and the church has been doing the same ever since.

Read through the whole book of Acts and you'll see that when people are cut by the Jesus story, they repent and are baptized. After hearing the message through a book, the Ethiopian man repents and is baptized (Acts 8). After hearing the message from God in prayer, Saul repents and is baptized (Acts 9). In Antioch, where followers of Jesus were first called Christians, we see the same (Acts 11). When Lydia (a citizen of Thyatira who heard Paul telling the story in Philippi) accepts the message, she and the members of her household are baptized (Acts 16), and the same is true for the jailer we read about later in that same chapter.

And the same continues to this day. Remember my friend Matthew, who grew up hating Christians and their silly T-shirts? Well, after hearing about Jesus himself, he was drawn to him and came to a point of wanting to respond to this news of Jesus he had heard. He had been intrigued by Jesus, he had become a Jesus fan, but in the end he knew that this news of Jesus and his kingdom demanded a whole-life response.

He didn't just want to admire Jesus and his dirty feet. He wanted to get his feet dirty too. And so when he asked me what it meant to respond to Jesus, I told him what Jesus had told the disciples, what Peter told the crowd that day and what the church has been calling people to ever since: repent and be baptized. And so he did. He placed his life under the reign of Jesus and was baptized.

Matthew knelt before Jesus in prayer while alone in his room and was later baptized in the freezing Boulder Reservoir. But that was Matthew. Since it's always individual people responding to that call, their repentance and baptism is always going to look a little different. That day in Jerusalem, there was little hesitation in Abram's response. Sometimes there's more hesitation. Matthew knew what the call was for several weeks before deciding to repent and be baptized. I've known people who have taken years to respond.

And in terms of baptism, there in Jerusalem most baptisms were done by completely immersing a person in water (like a stream or river), and many churches continue to do that today. (I've even heard of swimming pools being used at times!) Some churches build large basins so they can baptize people right there in their church building. Others pour the water or sprinkle it. There have been times when there was little water to be found and sand was used instead of water. All this variation shouldn't be too surprising—the call is to be baptized. That's what Jesus said. He didn't specify one particular way to perform that baptism.

Sometimes a person who has been baptized as an infant (a promissory baptism initiated by Christian parents) grows up and decides to follow Jesus, repenting and getting baptized again. Still others with a similar background have the same experience, except they don't get baptized again; they choose to say yes to their promissory baptism. They embrace it fully, thus fulfilling the promises that were made on their behalf years before.

Though the details have often looked different, the call is always the same as it was for Silas and Timon and the others: repent and be baptized.

THE PROMISE WAS CLEAR

Peter was also clear that day about what would happen if the people did repent and get baptized. They would be forgiven for their sins. And they would receive the gift of the Holy Spirit.

It had always been foretold that when the Messiah came he would make forgiveness possible. The prophet Isaiah (who lived more than seven hundred years before Jesus came) described the coming Messiah in this way:

Surely he took up our pain
*   and bore our suffering,*
yet we considered him punished by God,
*   stricken by him, and afflicted.*
But he was pierced for our transgressions,

he was crushed for our iniquities;
the punishment that brought us peace was on him,
   and by his wounds we are healed.
We all, like sheep, have gone astray,
   each of us has turned to his own way;
and the LORD has laid on him
   the iniquity of us all. (Isaiah 53:4-6)

These prophecies were fulfilled in Jesus. He came with for-giveness of sins. This message permeates his teachings.

The most famous of these teachings is the parable of the sinful son (found in Luke 15), where a son insults his father, sins against him and goes off into an unspeakably dirty life. And one day the son repents (changes his mind and turns around) and returns home, finding the arms of his father open and welcoming and full of forgiveness.

This message of forgiveness of sins also permeates the story of the torture and murder of Jesus. The story of what happened to Jesus in Jerusalem dominates each Gospel. It's the story of Jesus dying on the cross. And in the cross we have the fulfillment of that prophecy uttered by Isaiah, "The LORD has laid on him the iniquity of us all" (Isaiah 53:6). Jesus bore our sins that day. And made for-giveness possible for Hannah and Abram and all who turn to him.

No wonder the early church spoke so much, and in such moving ways, of the forgiveness of sins. Peter speaks of it constantly to the Jews: "All the prophets testify about him that everyone who believes in him receives forgiveness of sins through his name" (Acts 10:43). Paul speaks of it constantly in his sermons: "My brothers and sisters, I want you to know that through Jesus the forgiveness of sins is proclaimed to you" (Acts 13:38). And he writes eloquently of it in his letters: "He has rescued us from the dominion of darkness and brought us into the kingdom of the Son he loves, in whom we have redemption, the forgiveness of sins" (Colossians 1:13).

Jesus' church has been proclaiming that same promise ever since. But Peter made it clear to Silas and Miriam and the rest that *two* things would happen to them if they accepted the message. They would receive forgiveness for their sins. And they would receive "the gift of the Holy Spirit."

Again, Peter isn't making this up. This is exactly what Jesus himself had promised. After telling his first disciples that he would be leaving them one day (to ascend into heaven), Jesus told them what he would do next. "I will ask the Father, and he will give you another advocate to help you and be with you forever—the Spirit of truth. . . . You know him, for he lives with you and will be in you. I will not leave you as orphans; I will come to you" (John 14:16-18).

Jesus was clear that the Spirit would come and make a "home" within his followers, that the Spirit would remind his followers of all his words and teachings and that the Spirit would testify about Jesus (John 14:23, 25-26; 15:26). Jesus called the Spirit "the Advocate" (*paraclete* in Greek, meaning literally "one who comes alongside"). He is God's living presence in his people.

This is exactly what Peter had received that very day in Jerusalem. Jesus had told Peter and the others, "Do not leave Jerusalem, but wait for the gift my Father promised, which you have heard me speak about. . . . You will receive power when the Holy Spirit comes on you; and you will be my witnesses in Jerusalem, and in all Judea and Samaria, and to the ends of the earth" (Acts 1:4, 8).

And from this first sending of the Spirit on, we find out exactly why Jesus and everyone else kept referring to the Holy Spirit as a "gift." The Holy Spirit is a gift because this presence of God slowly changes people; they become more beautiful and humble and real. The Spirit begins to heal them, and that is a gift. As Paul later described this process, "The fruit of the Spirit is love, joy, peace, patience, kindness, goodness, faithfulness, gentleness and self-control. . . . Since we live by the Spirit, let us keep in step with the Spirit" (Galatians 5:22, 25).

This Spirit is a gift because he not only heals the soul but also gives "power," as Jesus had promised Peter and the others. As Paul describes it, "Now to each one the manifestation of the Spirit is given for the common good. To one there is given through the Spirit a message of wisdom, to another a message of knowledge by means of the same Spirit, to another faith by the same Spirit, to another gifts of healing by that one Spirit, to another miraculous powers, to another prophecy, to another distinguishing between spirits, to another speaking in different kinds of tongues, and to still another the interpretation of tongues. All these are the work of one and the same Spirit, and he distributes them to each one, just as he determines" (1 Corinthians 12:7-11).

Those last four words ("just as he determines") hint at another reason why it is appropriate to refer to the Holy Spirit as a "gift." The Spirit is given by God; the Spirit is not a possession. The Spirit is not something we can control or manipulate. The Spirit is not a tool. The Spirit is the presence of God. Try to control that gift (as Simon the sorcerer does in Acts 8) and you'll realize that it really is a gift—it can't be grabbed or purchased.

The Holy Spirit is a gift given *just as God determines.* There are no promises as to what that will be like or feel like. For some it is highly emotional; for others it is a whisper deep in their souls. For some it comes with explicit, physical manifestations; for others the changes are mental. It can't be labeled or parsed out or defined. It is mysterious and beautiful and intimate and personal and varies depending on what God determines.

My friend Matthew found himself (after repenting and being baptized) suddenly unable to continue mocking a student who was an outcast in his music department at school. He had always made fun of her. But after being reborn into the kingdom of Jesus, he began feeling compassion for her. Not only could he no longer treat her poorly, but he had an undeniable longing to serve her. That was a sure sign of the Spirit of God inside him. And that is a gift.

I have another friend, Cindy, who repented and was baptized. She loved her new life in Jesus' kingdom. And about two years after being baptized in Boulder Creek, while praying alone in her dorm room, she began inexplicably praying in another language. She didn't know the language, and she wasn't even sure she believed in speaking in tongues, but the words gave wings to the deepest prayers of her soul. That's a sure sign of the Spirit of God inside her. And that's a gift.

What this gift is like for your friends is no indication of what it will be like for you. What it means to have the Holy Spirit inside of you this year is no indication of what it will be like next year. What is sure, though, is what Peter told Abram and the rest: if you repent and are baptized, you will receive forgiveness of sins and the gift of the Holy Spirit.

THE BIG PICTURE WAS CLEAR

Peter was clear about the call that day in Jerusalem: repent and be baptized. And Peter was clear about what would happen if they did that: they would receive forgiveness for their sins and the gift of the Holy Spirit. But he was also clear about *why* any of that (the repenting, the baptizing, the forgiveness and the gift of the Spirit) would be happening in the first place: it was all because of God.

"The promise is for you and your children and all who are far off—for all *whom the Lord our God will call,*" Peter had said.

Peter pulled back the scope of perspective and provided a glimpse of the other side of the story that was going on. Why was there a loud noise coming from the Jesus followers? Why were they drawn as a crowd to the noise? Why did Peter tell the story, and why did it stab them so thoroughly in their hearts? And why would any of them actually repent and accept the message and be baptized into the church that day? Peter presents a huge, epic, mysterious answer: it's all happening because God is calling them into his kingdom.

This clearly doesn't mean that there is no real (and I mean *real*) choice on the part of Abram and Silas and Timon. It doesn't mean there aren't real struggles inside them, real decisions they are making, real emotions and thoughts and fears and hopes at play. In fact, we see in the next few verses that Peter isn't passive and calm in his call to them (as if they had no part in deciding). Rather we see that "with many other words he warned them; and he pleaded with them, 'Save yourselves from this corrupt generation' " (Acts 2:40).

Peter *pleads* with them. He *urges* them to save themselves. We see from this that it is up to them to decide. The people are doing it—they are the ones accepting the message. It is a clear act of volition.

But we also need to deal with the fact that Peter says the promise is for all whom *God will call.* We need to deal with the fact that when Jesus prayed to his Father he referred to his followers as "those whom *you gave me* out of the world" and "those *you have given* me" (John 17:6, 24, emphasis added). Paul himself states plainly that salvation "does not, therefore, depend on human desire or effort, but on God's mercy" (Romans 9:16).

As Acts goes on, we see people making decisions to accept the message and believe. But we are also shown God's hand in that. Remember Lydia from Thyatira? Well, we are told that "the Lord opened her heart to respond to Paul's message" before she and her household were baptized (Acts 16:14).

And thus the mystery. We see human choice urged and chosen and affirmed. And we see the sovereign, saving hand of God proclaimed in all its mercy and action on behalf of people. And that is a mystery.

For Silas and Timon the story is bigger than they might have thought. There is a side to it that had been going on all along and yet that they hadn't known anything about. It wasn't just the story of them finding God; it was also the story of God calling them. Peter affirms and clarifies both parts of the story and thus enters into this mysterious, grand story. What an oceanic story to proclaim!

I know that for me, as I was progressing toward my own conversion, it was very real and painful and confusing and joyful. I was full of debates and feelings and urges and questions. These were real and I will never forget them. The sleep I lost was real. The deep soul-calculations I was running were real—and were really painful to run. My journals from the time are full of questions and thoughts and ideas and, ultimately, decisions and choices, all scribbled in my messy, left-handed handwriting.

But as I look back now, I see a fuller story. It's not that I don't see all I was doing (I still have the journals!); it's just that I now see what God was up to at the time as well. How generous and active he was in my life. How sovereign he was over the circumstances. How his hand was at work in me and around me. How he was calling me to him.

And what a wonderful story to see! What a great truth to hold dearly—that God himself has pursued me! What has happened to me, and inside of me, is not a merely human act; it is also a divine act. I take Jesus' words to Nicodemus as great comfort—that only those who are born from the Spirit can enter his kingdom (John 3). I realize that, just as for a baby in the womb, there really was no way for me to give birth to myself. I needed the force of one greater than myself. I needed the gift of birth and life given to me. What a nearly unfathomable story to realize I am a part of!

Peter did want the crowd to know clearly what it meant to respond, but he also wanted them to know clearly what a merciful context they were making those decisions within. He invited them to stand in utter amazement at how present and active and intimate God himself was in their rebirth and in the grand story of their life.

WHAT ABOUT ME?

1. Know the clear call.

Abram and Hannah asked exactly what they should do. And Peter told them: repent and be baptized. That's the call. If you've heard something different about what the call to follow Jesus is, or about what it means to respond to the Jesus story, then you may have to adjust your assumptions a bit.

Some people may have heard much *less* about the call than what we see in our case study. I've met people who have spent time exploring Jesus and started going to church regularly, but they've never been told anything about baptism and so never planned on getting baptized. Clearly this ignores a central part of becoming a follower of Jesus.

I've met other people who have just heard about Jesus as a teacher. They study a few of his teachings and feel that they can respect Jesus and even incorporate some of his teachings into their life. But as we see in the life and words of Jesus himself, that is not an option, because Jesus wants *repentance.* He calls people to submit to his lordship and authority. He wants the whole person, and that is why the call to repentance is so important to grasp.

Repent and be baptized. It doesn't really get shorter than that. No response smaller than that is a response to the gospel.

Some people, though, have heard *more* than the call to repent and be baptized. They've been told that there's a much longer list of requirements for turning our lives over to Jesus.

For example, some people have been told that they don't just need to be baptized—they need to be baptized by a specific church. Or in a specific way. With a specific amount of water. Others have gotten the impression that they not only need to repent but also need to get some things straight in their life *first* in order for God to accept them or be pleased with them or to assure them of the forgiveness of their sins. If they want their repentance to "work," they assume, they must live a certain way or give a certain amount of money or look or pray or speak a certain way.

This is a pretty odd call, though, considering that it is repentance itself that ushers us into a land where change and renewal and the Holy Spirit are possible. It's silly to expect people who don't yet have the gift of the Holy Spirit to change themselves on the inside.

This is exactly why our case study is so helpful. Whether you've heard more or less than the call given to Abram and Hannah and the rest that day, this case study takes us back to the beginning to find out what it really means to become a Jesus follower. We, too, can know clearly what the call is.

2. Bask in the promises.

When we are talking about responding to the call of Jesus, we are talking about a real rebirth. It's the story of a birth that is nearly unthinkable for our jaded, cynical, entertainment-engorged minds to wrap around. Our eyes just aren't accustomed to opening this wide.

We are talking about oceanic realities like the forgiveness of all our deepest sins and stains. We are talking about the Holy Spirit of God, the very presence of the wild, free God of all creation, coming alongside us. We are talking about a Spirit who produces fruit within us— nearly unthinkable fruit such as self-control and kindness. We are talking about a Spirit who manifests gifts through us—such as healing and teaching and leading and speaking in tongues. That's what we're talking about.

When we talk about becoming a follower of Jesus,

and getting our feet dirty too, we are considering something so large and universal that it encircles both *our* actions (and thoughts and decisions and will) and the sovereign appointment *of God* (who calls all who will choose him).

So, if you are thoughtfully fingering the threads of this garment called Christian, wondering what it would be like to put it on and be "added to their number," then know the true epic nature of this rebirth you are considering. This is not a small story like trying on a new religion or taking on a new life philosophy or trying to be a better person or entering a social club. Know that what you are contemplating is so oceanic that you could pull and pull on the eyelids of your soul and still not open them wide enough to take in the full glory and full nature of these promises.

If you are wanting to read more about these promises, flip over to the first two chapters of the book called Ephesians in the New Testament. Ephesians is a short letter sent from Paul to various Jesus followers to help them celebrate more and more this new life they had found in Jesus. A fabulous read that proclaims and basks in the great realities of life as a follower of Jesus. Ephesians always seems to stretch my eyes wider, and I see a bit more of this immense story I am now a part of.

If you have become a follower of Jesus, then know fully and clearly what this new life is all about. The promises you see Peter proclaim over the crowd that day in Jerusalem are the very promises Jesus proclaims over you. You have received these gifts.

Bask in them. Contemplate them. Enjoy them. And know that this is the life God, in his great mercy, has granted to you.

the joy of being alive

Jesus said that he came to give an abundant life to his followers.

But how exactly did his earliest followers live?

And what would that look like today?

THE APOSTLES' TEACHING

playing a two-thousand-year-old game of telephone

At this point we are turning a corner. Our case study up to this point has been about the wonder of birth. We've watched Abram and Timon and Nicanor and Silas as they've been in the process of being born anew.

Now they are born. They are alive. And the second half of this book is dedicated to watching them be alive. What was it like for Azariah and Miriam to live their days now that they were born anew? What was it like for them to have Jesus as their King, to live with forgiven sins, to have the Spirit of Jesus living inside them?

Those who accepted his message were baptized, and about three thousand were added to their numbers that day.

They devoted themselves to the apostles' teaching and to fellowship, to the breaking of bread and to prayer. Everyone was filled with awe at the many won-

ders and miraculous signs done by the apostles. All the believers were together and had everything in common. They sold property and possessions to give to anyone who had need. Every day they continued to meet together in the temple courts. They broke bread in their homes and ate together with glad and sincere hearts, praising God and enjoying the favor of all the people. And the Lord added to their number daily those who were being saved. (Acts 2:41-47)

One of the most striking aspects of life for Timon and Nicanor is found in three words: "they devoted themselves." After repentance and baptism, there was devotion.

The word used in the original Greek for devotion is *proskarterountes.* It comes from two Greek words being put together: *pros,* which means "toward" and has an intensifying connotation to it, and *karteros,* which means "strong." Literally meaning "being strong toward," *proskarterountes* carries the connotation of continuing steadfastly in something. It is often translated "persevere in."

Devotion is a specific phenomenon. It's something like discipline and love wrapped together into one strong, simple, willful state of attention toward something. It is meaningful that this is the first word used to describe Silas and his friends after they were reborn.

But what exactly were they devoted to? Not surprisingly, the four things they were "strong toward"—the apostles' teaching, fellowship, the breaking of bread and prayer—are all things that Jesus had explicitly called his followers to be about. These four activities were a central part of their new life.

We'll take the next four chapters to examine each of these four devotions in turn, beginning in this chapter with the teaching of the apostles. What exactly were the apostles teaching? And what did it mean to be devoted to that? And what would devotion to the teaching look like today?

THE APOSTLES' TEACHING IS ALL ABOUT JESUS

All you have to do is read the sermons and letters of the apostles (the very first Jesus-followers) to find out exactly what they were teaching. And what you find, again not surprisingly, is that their teaching was all about Jesus. He was the center of their message.

They talked all about who he was and what he did and what he taught. They talked about his life and his torturous death and his coming to life again. They repeated all his parables and his promises and his interactions with people. They talked about what he said about repentance and baptism and the Holy Spirit and forgiveness of sins. They talked about how the Hebrew Scriptures were fulfilled by the coming of Jesus the Messiah. They talked about the kind of King he was.

Well, before ascending into heaven and sending his Spirit to his followers, Jesus had given his followers some specific instructions: "Go and make disciples of all nations, baptizing them in the name of the Father and of the Son and of the Holy Spirit, and teaching them to obey everything I have commanded you" (Matthew 28:19-20). They were supposed to teach new followers everything Jesus had taught them.

"You will be my witnesses," Jesus had also said to them (for example, Acts 1:8). They had seen something (Jesus) and were now to be witnesses of what they had seen. That's why the apostles' teaching was all about Jesus.

And Jesus promised to help them with this simple act of witnessing about him, the King. He promised them, "When the Advocate comes, whom I will send to you from the Father—the Spirit of truth who goes out from the Father—he will testify about me. And you also must testify, for you have been with me from the beginning" (John 15:26-27).

So the apostles testified about Jesus. And Silas and his friends were devoted to hearing that testimony. They were devoted to hearing about Jesus—about his life and teachings and death and parables and resurrection and miracles and . . . and all of it. And when you read the rest of Acts, you can see that this is exactly what they *were* being taught. And when you read the letters the apostles wrote to new followers of Jesus, you can see the same.

But all this teaching about Jesus wasn't just to satisfy people's curiosity; it was to bring them life. Jesus had taught clearly that hearing *and obeying* his words leads to a solid, sure, real life. Simply hearing (but not obeying) his words leads to shaky ground and in the end is foolish (see Luke 6:46-49).

So the apostles taught about Jesus, and the new Jesus followers were devoted to hearing about Jesus because that is where they found life. We could learn from their simplicity and focus.

When I was a young follower of Jesus, I became interested in Old Testament prophecies and Revelation images and how those were (or were not) being fulfilled in the Cold War that was on the front page of the paper every day. I found this intriguing, mysterious and titillating. Was Gorbachev the Antichrist? Were the latest troop movements in Russia indications that the end times were finally upon us? I even wrote my senior high school English thesis on the fact that the world was about to end, as indicated in recent events. This was in the spring of 1990.

While all this study had me reading the Bible regularly, it wasn't a very fruitful reading. I had been sucked into a silly code-word game that happened to involve the Bible but that had nothing to do with sitting under the clear teachings of the Bible. This is not to say that reading Isaiah or Revelation or studying about Jesus' words on his sure second coming are to be avoided. This is just to say that I could have learned from young Silas and bearded Abram by making sure I was devoting myself, quite specifically, to the apostles' teaching: hearing about Jesus, studying his life and his teachings, learning how to obey the clear things he taught.

The more I have done this, the more I have found out what those three thousand Jesus followers discovered and what Jesus himself promised: that hearing of Jesus and obeying his words leads to fruit that lasts. And leads to a solid life.

THE APOSTLES' TEACHING IS A RECEIVED MESSAGE

It's important to note that Hannah and Nicanor and the rest were specifically devoted to a message that the apostles had *received* and were plainly *passing on.* They were not devoting themselves to any ideas that these apostles themselves had come up with on their own. This is an important distinction. A distinction the apostles were careful to make clear while they were teaching.

As John wrote, he made this clear. "That which was from the beginning, which we have heard, which we have seen with our eyes, which we have looked at and our hands have touched—this we proclaim concerning the Word of life. The life appeared; we have seen it and testify to it. . . . We proclaim to you what we have seen and heard" (1 John 1:1-3).

Peter wasn't quite as poetic as John, but he was just as careful to make the same point about where his message was coming from. "We did not follow cleverly devised stories when we told you about the coming of our Lord Jesus Christ in power, but we were eyewitnesses of his majesty" (2 Peter 1:16).

This is the story all the apostles made clear: we received this from Jesus, and so we are passing it on to you. In fact, that has been the posture of the church from generation to generation. The church echoes the refrain of Paul: "What I received I passed on to you" (1 Corinthians 15:3).

The received nature of the message is significant because it makes it possible to distinguish between the apostles' teaching (received from Jesus) and false teaching (not received from Jesus). False teachings come from folks who, for whatever reason, don't receive and pass on the message of Jesus.

Just consider some of the earliest descriptions of these false teachers: "They are from the world and therefore speak from the viewpoint of the world, and the world listens to them" (1 John 4:5). "In their greed these teachers will exploit you with fabricated stories" (2 Peter 2:3). "See to it that no one takes you captive through hollow and deceptive philosophy, which depends on human tradition and the elemental spiritual forces of this world rather than on Christ" (Colossians 2:8).

By contrast, teachers in the church were encouraged, "Guard the good deposit that was entrusted to you— guard it with the help of the Holy Spirit who lives in us. . . . The things you have heard me say in the presence of many witnesses entrust to reliable people who will also be qualified to teach others" (2 Timothy 1:14; 2:2).

Isn't that a clear distinction? True teachers are marked by the fact that they receive the message that originated with Jesus and repeat it faithfully. False teach- ers are marked by the fact that they are making up ideas or speaking from the common sense of the world. Strong, bearded Abram and the rest didn't need more made-up ideas or more common sense; they wanted to hear about *Jesus,* to learn what *he* taught and what *he* did and what *he* made clear for them. That's what they were devoting themselves to.

As a young Jesus follower, I was glad to receive the message. But a strange thing happened the first time I was asked to do a small teaching at a Young Life retreat on the Oregon coast: I felt I had to come up with some- thing. Something clever and meaningful and helpful to say to the rest of the high schoolers at the camp. I became stressed over this prospect and tried with all my human abilities to come up with something meaningful to say.

This temptation was a silly one. As a follower of Jesus,

I follow one who has all the ideas. He is the King; I am not. There's no pressure on me to be clever. I am simply to repeat what Jesus taught and has been passed down to me. I am to be a witness.

As I've taught more and more over the years, though, this subtle temptation to come up with something new and clever and witty continues to tug at me. Even though followers of Jesus have a *received* message, the world expects something new and flashy and original.

This is why our case study is so helpful. It reminds us of the original nature of the apostles' teaching. Teachers in the church are not charged with the task of coming up with some new ideas or of recommending their way of seeing the world to others. Rather they are charged with repeating what they have clearly received. And there is great freedom in that. We have only one King, Jesus.

This is precisely why I am closely following Acts 2 in writing this book and why you see cross-references to the Gospels and Epistles on practically every page. I'm not in the business of coming up with new things to recommend to the curious and convinced; I'm in the business of receiving and passing on the teachings of Jesus as preserved through the apostles' teaching.

Just as the three thousand new Jesus followers were devoted to this message of Jesus that was being handed down from generation to generation, so we, too, can be devoted to the exact same message, which is still being received and passed on to this very day.

THE APOSTLES' TEACHING IS SCRIPTURE

But how can we be sure that the message, after more than two thousand long years of being received and passed on, is still the same message that Silas and the rest heard there in Jerusalem? How can we be sure that message hasn't been distorted as the church plays a two-thousand-year-long game of Telephone?

We can be sure because the teachings of the apostles (those first-generation, eyewitness Jesus followers) were written down.

Remember, Jesus had explicitly promised that the Holy Spirit would guide the apostles as they testified about Jesus (John 15:26-27). And the Spirit led them to record for all time their eyewitness accounts. This would allow followers of Jesus for the next two thousand years to have a written copy of the message that they could continue to devote themselves to. Having this permanent record allows Christians of each new generation to make sure that their own teaching remains a faithful repeating of that message.

Now, the apostles already had a spiritual text: the Hebrew Scriptures. Jesus himself clearly saw the Hebrew Bible as from God. He studied it from an early age, quoted from it often, and defended it strongly. In fact, when Jesus was accused of abandoning the Hebrew Scriptures, he responded, "Do not think that I have come to abolish the Law or the Prophets; I have not come to abolish them but to fulfill them. Truly I tell you, until heaven and earth disappear, not the smallest letter, not the least stroke of a pen, will by any means disappear from the Law" (Matthew 5:17-18).

If you have more detailed questions about the New Testament and how it was written and collected, I highly recommend that you read the works of scholars who are experts in these historical, literary matters. For example, read F. F. Bruce's *The New Testament Documents: Are They Reliable?* 6th ed. (InterVarsity Press, 2003).

The Hebrew Scriptures were written by humans under the guidance of God. Jesus believed this. And he also believed (as he explicitly claimed) that he had been sent by God to *fulfill* those Scriptures. He fulfilled them with his life and teachings and death and resurrection and founding of the church. And so, when the apostles testified about Jesus (and his message and life and death and resurrection), their testimony was written down and became the fulfillment, or conclusion, to those Hebrew Scriptures. This second book came to be known as the New Testament.

That New Testament, and the Hebrew Scriptures that led up to it (which came to be called the Old Testament), form what is known today simply as the Bible. Which literally means "the Book." Quite a title for a book, huh? A fitting title, because it is not just any old book; it is the truth that came from God, that was fulfilled in Jesus and that was testified to by the earliest apostles.

So when we devote ourselves to the Bible, we are doing the same thing Silas and his friends did when they devoted themselves to the apostles' teaching.

I have a long history with the Bible, a history that is much longer than my life as a Christian. I grew up with Bibles in my house and found their impossibly thin pages and gold edges and pitch-black covers to be at once imposing and intriguing. When I read the Bible as a young boy, it was always in secret, as someone might read a book of magic spells hidden away in an attic.

But this early reverence for the Bible changed as I grew older and started reading other intriguing books and found the Bible less interesting. And so my posture toward the Bible changed, and I only used it to . . . well, impress girls. Try to impress girls, anyway. For some reason I felt that sprinkling my language from time to time with a deep-sounding quote from Proverbs might make me sound clever and interesting and increase my chances with the beautiful but scary female creatures who glided through the halls of my high school. All to no avail. So I stopped reading the Bible altogether.

And then I became a Christian. And all of a sudden I was told that this same book—once so mysterious and then so utilitarian and finally so irrelevant—was a book I should take great interest in and even *devote* myself to reading. At first I was skeptical. This book and I had a history, none of which led me to believe that reading it could be as amazing as everyone insisted.

But then I started reading it. I was reading many parts of it *again*, but in reality I was reading it all for the first time. For in it I found him. My Jesus. The one I had left everything to follow—his very words and the details of his life were there. And all of a sudden my reading of this book became an intimate thing. Here was the message of my King, the stories of the one who was now the center of my life.

And over time, as I have devoted myself to reading it, I feel what I imagine the disciples must have felt when sitting at the feet of Jesus: a deep, sober sense of what a gift it is to be hearing what I'm hearing.

Jesus fulfilled his promise that his Spirit would guide the church in testifying about him. Because of God's choice to have the Bible recorded, we can still devote ourselves, just like Abram and Hannah, to the apostles' teaching.

WHAT ABOUT ME?
1. Devote yourself to reading the Bible.

We're told in our case study that these new Christians were meeting every day in order to hear the teachings of the apostles. So there's a great precedent for hearing the message over and over again and for doing that on a fairly regular basis.

This doesn't mean you need to read the Bible ecstatically or brilliantly or with never-ebbing enthusiasm. It just means you should be reading it. And reading it regularly. Of course, reading it with an eye for obeying is the kind of posture that Jesus said would be fruitful.

So we read regularly. We read to hear from Jesus, to have his Spirit testify to our souls about him, to hear the difference between the truth of Jesus and the common sense of the world around us. When we read the Bible, it is like we are sitting in the dirt at Jesus' feet and getting to hear what he has to say to us.

In terms of what parts of the Bible to read, you can never really go wrong. But there is some wise counsel I've received along the way. Try to read from both the Old and the New Testaments, and try to pick a nice size to focus on—it's kind of like food: you want to bite off enough to chew and swallow without choking on the one hand or going hungry on the other. And try to read it with other people on a regular basis—this always seems to lead to more fruitful, accurate, enjoyable reading.

And try to remember to always read *in context.* I'm not sure why random-sentence reading (a foolish reading strategy no matter what you are trying to read) is used with the Bible, but it is. Try not to get into the habit yourself. Always ask two questions when reading the Bible. First ask: What did this mean back then? Then (and only then) you can ask the second question: What does this mean for me?

There's plenty of other stuff we could say about reading the Bible. But suffice it to say that your reading of the Bible will certainly grow and evolve and mature over time. Take that developmental perspective with you as you attend to reading the Bible, just like those three thousand there in Jerusalem.

2. Devote yourself to sitting under the apostles' teaching at a church near you.

When I became a follower of Jesus, I eventually took to reading the Bible with gusto, but it never occurred to me that I should go to church.

A great place to start growing your reading of the Bible (other than just starting to read the thing!) would be getting a copy of *How to Read the Bible for All Its Worth* by Fee and Stuart (Zondervan, 2003) or *Transforming Bible Study* by Bob Grahmann (InterVarsity Press, 2003). Both of these books have helped me read the Bible more thoughtfully, intelligently and fruitfully. I recommend them both highly.

I'm not exactly sure why it never occurred to me (I have my hunches), but I do know that it was a few months before someone asked me why I wasn't going to a church. I didn't have a good reason (other than some residual resistance I had from growing up), so I started going to church.

The great thing about that was that I learned what a gift it is to sit under the teaching of a pastor and hear a talk about Jesus. This is what Hannah and the rest felt, I'm sure: the joy of sitting under the teaching of someone who had received the message of Jesus and was passing it on to another generation of Jesus followers. This message had changed my life, and it was great to hear that message talked about and explained and celebrated. And it made sense to devote myself to that.

And it has taken real devotion. Because it hasn't necessarily come easily or without effort. There are lots of things I could be doing with my Sunday mornings: sleeping in, watching football games on TV, getting the house squared away before another week crashes over me . . .

But once I started tasting the fruits of getting to hear about Jesus, I realized why devotion doesn't just mean discipline but is a sort of discipline wrapped in love. Because I find life as I get to hear the apostolic teaching repeated. Jesus is spoken into my life in new ways every week.

Now, a couple of warnings are in order in regard to

going to church. First, you need to know that there can be a tendency for Jesus followers to find themselves getting together all the time. This, in and of itself, isn't necessarily bad, but if it starts to feel like an exclusive social club, you run the temptation of losing sight of *why* you are all getting together (Jesus). Also, getting together all the time with other Jesus followers *exclusively* could distance you unnecessarily from your friends and family. You likely won't run into this, but it's important to know the temptation is there.

The second warning about devoting yourself to a church is that not all churches are repeating the apostles' teaching. For a variety of reasons, some churches stray from the apostolic message about Jesus (as preserved in the Bible and passed down through the centuries) and instead stray into other messages. Don't let the cross on the steeple deceive you—not all churches will talk about Jesus as he is talked about in the pages of the New Testament. As you start going to church, you need to know that.

The last thing I want to do is make you hypersensitive and cynical going into a church. The reality is that nearly all of those churches whose steeples are topped with crosses have received the same message that Hannah and Nicanor and Timon heard and are passing it on just like Peter and John and Paul did. Odds are, you're going to be fine.

But just know that if you find yourself in a church

where the name of Jesus doesn't come up every week, you might want to ask some questions. And if you're in a church where the Bible is not taught from often, you also might want to ask some questions.

But most likely, you're going to find a wonderful place full of imperfect, dirty-footed Jesus followers (just like you) where you can receive the good deposit week after week, basking in the telling of the story of Jesus and being encouraged in your own new life with him. Devote yourself to this and you will never regret it.

THE FELLOWSHIP

the spirituality of the kitchen table

Like newborn babies, Silas and Abram and the rest of the three thousand were starting a brand-new life. And the first details we're given about their new life is that they became people of devotion. In the last chapter we looked at their new devotion to the apostles' teaching and all that meant for them. In this chapter we take up their second devotion.

They devoted themselves to the apostles' teaching and to fellowship, to the breaking of bread and to prayer. Everyone was filled with awe at the many wonders and miraculous signs done by the apostles. All the believers were together and had everything in common. They sold property and possessions to give to anyone who had need. Every day they continued to meet together in the temple courts. They broke bread in their homes and ate together with glad and sincere hearts, praising God and enjoying the favor of all the people. And the Lord added to their number daily those who were being saved. (Acts 2:42-47)

They devoted themselves to fellowship. The original Greek word for fellowship is *koinonia.* The root of this Greek word is *koinos,* which literally means "common." So this state of koinonia can be (and has been) translated as "partnership," as "fellowship" and even as "communion." It's the idea of sharing in common. In other words, Abram and Azariah and Timon were devoted to being in common with each other.

In verses 42-47 of our case study in Acts 2 there are a variety of details that shed light on what this communing was like. They met daily in the temple courts; they ate in each other's homes; they had glad and sincere hearts as they ate together. Now, we could go on to even more interesting expressions of their fellowship (such as sharing their money and possessions!), but it's plenty interesting to stop and recognize just how intimate this table fellowship was.

In the culture of that time and place, to share some-one's table was a sign of commitment, of intimacy. And these new Christians were in each other's homes, at each other's tables regularly. Even today we still have some re-sidual sense of how intimate it is to sit inside someone's home, at the table with their family. It's one thing to meet in a safe third-party location (such as a coffee shop) but quite another to have others come into your home, where they can see all of who you are, your family, the pictures on the wall, your laundry on the floor . . .

Nicanor and Silas and the other new followers of Jesus were devoted to this intimate, real kind of communing together. They were strongly attentive to fellowship. And their experience tells us a lot about fellowship in the life of a new Christian.

FELLOWSHIP IS CENTRAL

The communal life of Nicanor and the others was not an anomaly. They were following Jesus, which meant living a life with people.

Jesus himself had lived this way. He called disciples to follow him. Which meant they ate together and traveled together and lived together and worked together. And Jesus called his disciples to live the same kind of life with others. "My command is this," he said: "Love each other as I have loved you" (John 15:12). It's always about relationships, according to Jesus. No one is to be an island.

One time Jesus was asked what the greatest commandment of all the Hebrew Scriptures was. His response? "'Love the Lord your God with all your heart and with all your soul and with all your mind.' This is first and greatest commandment. And the second is like it: 'Love your neighbor as yourself.' All the Law and Prophets hang on these two commandments" (Matthew 22:37-40).

Jesus taught that *all of life* hangs on a loving relationship with God (first and foremost) and loving relationships with the silly people who are right next to us. Jesus insists that this is the point of our lives here on earth, even for stiff academic types (see his interaction with a lawyer in Luke 10:25-37!). He teaches that humans are the most valuable thing in the universe (by far) and that this should make a difference in our days on this earth (Mark 8:36).

This theme is unavoidable in the teachings of Jesus and in the life he lived. People are infinitely valuable to Jesus. So it should come as no great surprise that when rough, bearded Abram repented of his former life and was baptized into Jesus' kingdom he became a man devoted to fellowship. And it shouldn't be too surprising if we see the same thing happening today.

One of my dearest mentors, Thomas, was a self-proclaimed elitist while growing up. He was used to floating in certain social circles and looked down on people who weren't "quality people." This was before he ran into Jesus. When he first got familiar with Jesus and his teachings, he began to realize what a profound, over-arching claim it was that within Jesus' kingdom people were of infinite value. My friend knew that this was not his view. And he knew implicitly that to enter this kingdom would mean shedding his social habits and taking on a new commitment to fellowship.

When he repented and was baptized, he did just that. In fact, he became so devoted to fellowship, to the people he ran into from day to day, that his life as a Jesus follower has been sacrificially, beautifully, joyfully lived in deep fellowship. His home has practically had a revolving door for decades now as hundreds of friends, travelers, students and (especially) the homeless have found their way into their crazy, welcoming home. Their kitchen table has had thousands of elbows rest on it.

Once we enter into Jesus' kingdom, we are in a land where fellowship is central. There's no more living in small bubbles, isolated from others.

In our case study we see that Timon and the others were "enjoying the favor of all the people." This means they weren't hiding away to privately practice their religion, but rather they were living life naturally right there in the midst of all the folks in Jerusalem. It wasn't a bubble religion; it was a street faith—happening right there as they walked around.

FELLOWSHIP IS A BLESSING

Not only is fellowship *central* to the life of a Jesus follower; it is a huge gift.

There is something beautiful about fellowship. Psalm 133 (one of the shorter psalms) is a testimony to this beauty:

How good and pleasant it is
   when God's people live together in unity!

It is like precious oil poured on the head,
   running down on the beard,
running down on Aaron's beard,
   down on the collar of his robe.
It is as if the dew of Hermon
   were falling on Mount Zion.
For there the LORD bestows his blessing,
   even life forevermore. (Psalm 133)

Now, some of the psalmist's images and metaphors may be lost on us (oil running down onto my beard is good?), but the sense of the psalm is clear: when people dwell together, when they live in communion, it is a great thing. It is beautiful.

There's strength in numbers ("Though one may be overpowered, two can defend themselves. A cord of three strands is not quickly broken," Ecclesiastes 4:12). And fellowship ensures that the vulnerable are cared for ("They sold property and possessions to give to anyone who had need," Acts 2:45). But even more importantly, this call to live life communally (among and for others) turns out to be a blessing for everyone, especially those who are sacrificing for others.

After washing his disciples' dirty feet (yuck), Jesus told the disciples that if they did the same to each other they would receive blessings. "Now that you know these things, you will be blessed if you do them" (John 13:17).

If you love others, he says, you will be *blessed.* The word in the original Greek comes from a root word meaning "large" or "lengthy." To be blessed is to find yourself happy or large. Jesus says that if we live communally, loving those we are near, we will find this spiritual largeness flowing into us. No wonder they had such glad and sincere hearts.

The blessing of fellowship has surprised me deeply over the years. I was not set up to assume that communing with others would be a good thing. I'm a so-called introvert, which means I grew up playing by myself and was quite content with this. For much of my life I have fantasized about living alone in a cabin in the woods. Ah, the cabin in the woods. All alone with a basketball hoop, a dog, endless books and miles of wilderness surrounding me. I'd be in heaven, pure heaven.

But when I became a follower of Jesus, this fantasy started to erode. I found myself living in a land where people were important, where God loved people sacrificially (getting his feet dirty in the everyday grime of life) and where he kept gently nudging me to do the same.

I initially obeyed like a dutiful son eating his vegetables. But over time I started to feel . . . well, *large.* Blessed. I felt closer to Jesus. I felt more alive. I felt genuine affection for people growing within me. And now, after a decade of a relationally intense vocation and a decade of marriage to an extrovert who keeps our kitchen table full of people, I realize just how right Jesus was. I have learned what it means to eat with others with a glad and sincere heart.

I never knew life could feel like this. I had no idea. And I am indebted to Jesus for being wiser than me and for calling me to get my feet dirty in this wonderful world of people.

And it's a good thing following Jesus has me so enamored with messy, wonderful fellowship: it turns out that's where I'm heading. It turns out heaven, as described in the Bible, isn't some rolling countryside where estates are nicely fenced off and everyone has elbow room. In the book of Revelation heaven is described with one resounding, perhaps surprising word: *city* (see Revelation 21:2, for example).

Heaven is a city. It's the culmination of what we're created for as humans: blessed fellowship.

FELLOWSHIP IS COSTLY

Fellowship is central to life with Jesus, and it is a source of extreme, lasting, sometimes mysterious blessings. But we must not overlook the fact that it is supremely and unmistakably costly.

Just in the few details we've seen thus far in our case study, we know that living in common with others costs time and money and emotions. Abram, Timon and Nicanor were spending liberally from their Day-Timers, wallets and hearts. And I don't think I have to point out that those can be some costly places to spend from. Often our natural instincts would have us protect and guard those precious resources, not spend them on others.

Jesus says that we are blessed when we wash each other's feet, but we can't ignore the fact that washing feet is humbling and dirty and awkward. Jesus says that we find greatness when we become the servant of others (Matthew 20:26), but being a servant involves actions of the utmost self-denial. Jesus celebrates the mystery that we are dwelling richly with him when we care for the marginalized and forgotten who have no one else to care for them (Matthew 25:35-40), but caring for those who have no one usually involves going way out of our way, which means setting our own agendas aside for a time.

Let there be no mistaking this truth—being devoted to fellowship is costly.

Several years ago I was trying to love my neighbors in a dorm near my apartment. I was trying to foster community in a place where community is rare. One freshman, Dan, seemed excited to be devoted to fellowship in the dorm and so we started meeting regularly. We didn't meet in the temple like the three thousand; we tended to go to Denny's. Being devoted to fellowship together over the next five years was amazing: we prayed together, hiked together, ate together, started an inner-city ministry together, ran camps together, lived together, cleaned bathrooms together . . .

Dan came to the hospital when my first son was born. I cried with Dan through the ups and downs of dating relationships. Dan came to the hospital when my daughter was born. My wife and I did premarriage counseling with Dan and his girlfriend. Dan cried with me when life was hard. We were devoted to fellowship with each other, Dan and I. And that was beautiful. One of the best things I've ever done with my life.

But it was also costly. You can ask Dan and I'm sure he'll tell you the same thing. We gave up many things to be with each other; we became emotionally involved in each other's pains and struggles; we fought with each other and had disagreements; we let each other down; we had to ask for forgiveness. And reconcile. Being in fellowship with each other was messy and wonderful and cost us each dearly.

But that's the only kind of fellowship there is— fellowship that costs you something. That's why, I think, Abram and Miriam were *devoted* to it, not just casually trying it on for size. Because something real and deep and beautiful and costly and blessed like fellowship doesn't come overnight. It comes through devotion. And is always worth it.

WHAT ABOUT ME?

1. Devote yourself to temple fellowship.

While the word *church* has taken on many connotations over the years, it's really just about Jesus followers being plural. Church is what Silas was experiencing there in Jerusalem. And it is something every new Christian should be devoted to as well.

This most obviously means finding a church and becoming a part of it. Attend the weekly worship service where the apostles' teaching is repeated and where you can pray with other believers. Perhaps attend a Bible study or small group. Start getting in common with others.

There are a number of ways you can be devoted to a fellowship of believers, and they all involve . . . well, being together with others. No rocket science here. There's no special koinonia pill you can take. There's nothing magical and quick a church can do to bring you into the fellowship. It's about relationships, after all. And those take time. And investment. So be about that.

A word of counsel as you look to devote yourself to fellowship with a body of believers: don't look for the perfect church. You'll never find it.

Of course you will want to find a church that in some sense suits you. That's for sure. But be wary of giving into a blatantly consumeristic posture that only looks at what a church has to offer you. The church is not an outlet mall with various enticements to draw you in, exchanging their goods for your cash. The church is a body of believers. Find a body and attach yourself to it. And be devoted to that attachment.

Paul takes this body language to the next level. "Just as a body, though one, has many parts, but all its many parts form one body, so it is with Christ. For we were all baptized by one Spirit so as to form one body. . . . The body is not made up of one part but of many" (1 Corinthians 12:12-14).

We are not consumers coming to a store, Paul says; we are body parts that are integral parts of the church body. We are each a part (an ear, an eye, the nose, a foot), and church is those parts coming together to form a viable body (see 1 Corinthians 12:15-31). So just pick a church and attach yourself to it. An ear floating around by itself doesn't make sense. Don't allow your church browsing to keep you from just choosing a body and putting your ear in the mix.

When I moved to Boulder, Colorado, my wife and I chose to become members of the first church we were invited to. At first I was enamored with this new church and how we did worship and teaching and Communion and all. But over the years there have been long seasons of disenchantment (my vocation has me visiting other churches from time to time, and my consumeristic posture starts to kick in) as well as seasons of outright frustration with my church. But in the end I'm glad we've stayed there, practicing the refreshing discipline of stability.

I'm glad we've stayed because I know that while the grass may look greener somewhere else, if we moved we'd eventually find a third patch of grass to start pining for. I'm glad we've stayed, because our time there has been rich in blessings and devoted relationships that we never would have had were we to keep moving to different churches. We've done life with this body of believers and have experienced truth and love and reconciliation and celebration and boredom and surprise and longing and tragedy. And we've done all that together. And that's what fellowship (and life, as it turns out) is all about.

In the end I'm glad we've stayed because it seems that that's the whole point of being devoted to fellowship: Being devoted. To fellowship. That's the life Silas started living after his conversion, and it's the life we can live today as well.

2. Devote yourself to table fellowship.

While it is certainly true (and wonderful) that Silas and Hannah and Nicanor were meeting together in the temple, we must not allow ourselves to assume that being all together in one place is the end all and be all of fellowship.

We see quite clearly in our increasingly helpful case study that these followers of Jesus were also meeting in each other's homes. Having meals together. Sharing table fellowship.

There are some things you can accomplish only when everyone is in a room together—everyone worshiping and praying together, hearing the same teaching, celebrating events as a body. But there are also things you can accomplish only while sitting at someone's kitchen table. In this more intimate setting, with fewer people, you can experience extended conversation and heart-to-heart relating; you can provide encouragement to one person or receive counsel from someone who knows you well; you can have friends who actually know the details of your life, and you can know what's important to someone else.

This intimate table fellowship is an essential part of true fellowship. And as such is something we should be devoted to.

Now, this can take a variety of forms, from an accountability group of peers, to a home group with other families, to a weekly mentoring relationship, to a couple of close friends you see on a regular basis, to people you invite out to lunch after church each Sunday, to a night of the week when you share dinner with another family or group of people from your church or neighborhood, to organized ministry teams, to a rotating community dinner schedule, to small groups, to support groups, to the many other forms that have already jumped into your head while reading this paragraph!

The form isn't as important as the principle that we

see lived out in our case study: table fellowship is different from temple fellowship, and we need both.

The truth is that some of us are more attracted to temple fellowship. We like being in big groups and the teaching that goes on there. And perhaps we like the relative anonymity that comes with being in a room full of people. For us, table fellowship is a bit scary. It's a little too intimate, a little too inefficient, a little too in-your-face. So we get subtle in how we hide from true table fellowship: we give a nice answer rather than tell the truth about how we're doing; we rush back to the nursery to get our kids rather than have to talk with other adults; we comment on the banalities of life rather than ask how our neighbor is doing—and really mean it when we ask.

If you're looking to grow your own life of table fellowship, read *The Pursuit of God in the Company of Friends* by Richard Lamb (InterVarsity Press, 2003). This book has been a tremendous help to me as I have sought to be devoted to fellowship—and continues to be helpful every time I return to it.

For us, we need to be reminded that in the land of Jesus there is no need for these hiding techniques. There's no need to import our worldly games into his kingdom. His kingdom is a land of honesty, of confession, of truth speaking and of real-life people—messy, inefficient and awkward though they may be. And we need to devote ourselves to table fellowship.

But there are others of us who are enamored with table fellowship. We like this intimate encounter so much that we ignore temple fellowship. We're the ones who love having an audience, love being fed, love all those listening ears. We're the ones who become reliant on human relationships to such an extent that we are in danger of dethroning Jesus and replacing him with our mentors and supportive friends. Going to church becomes a time for making our needs known and getting invited to lunch, not for breathing in the truth of the apostles' teaching or for praying to our high and mighty God.

For us, we need to be reminded that the first great commandment is to love God with all that we are. And that the second (yes, *second*) is to love our neighbors. We must be wary of eschewing temple fellowship and allowing our souls to become so needy and grabby that we enter into table fellowship in an unhealthy, selfish way.

The good news is that the Spirit of God is within us, slowly redeeming our hurts and fears, teaching us how to more fully breathe in all the joys of fellowship. In the meantime the point for all of us is to be devoted, in healthy ways, to table fellowship. To be *devoted* to it. It doesn't come easily or naturally for all of us, and that's where the devotion comes in.

THE BREAKING OF BREAD

So far, we know that Hannah and the rest were devoted to the apostles' teaching and devoted to fellowship. But that's not all. They were also devoted to a little thing called the breaking of bread. Seems like an innocent enough thing, kind of domestic sounding. But it was something so significant that Hannah was careful to always be strong toward it.

They devoted themselves to the apostles' teaching and to fellowship, to the breaking of bread and to prayer. (Acts 2:42)

The breaking of bread is rooted in history. You see, on the Thursday night before the weekend of his death and resurrection, Jesus ate a Passover meal with his closest followers. They had all traveled to Jerusalem for the celebration of Passover, along with thousands of other Jews, and they were eating their Passover meal in the upper room of a house, reclining together at a low table.

Passover was a celebration instituted by God to help the Jews remember how he had delivered them from destruction and freed them from Egyptian slavery (see Exodus 12). On the original Passover day God had instructed the Hebrews to smear the blood of a lamb onto their doorposts as a sign of their relationship to God, so that the plague of death would pass over their house.

And so Jews for centuries celebrated Passover, including the Passover meal, which always involved bread and wine. The meal was a reenactment of sorts, a sign of solidarity. As they ate, they were remembering and proclaiming, *"We, too,* were captives. *We, too,* were set free."

It was this meal that Jesus and his followers were eating when Jesus all of a sudden veered from the standard Passover rituals. "When the hour came, Jesus and his apostles reclined at the table. And he said to them, 'I have eagerly desired to eat this Passover with you before I suffer. For I tell you, I will not eat it again until it finds fulfillment in the kingdom of God' " (Luke 22:14-16).

While the disciples probably weren't sure exactly what Jesus meant *(What suffering is he talking about? And how can Passover be "fulfilled" in this kingdom of his?),* they definitely were catching on that this was going to be a different Passover meal. And it was.

Paul summarizes what happened at this Last Supper this way: "The Lord Jesus, on the night he was betrayed, took bread, and when he had given thanks, he broke it and said, 'This is my body, which is for you; do this in remembrance of me.' In the same way, after supper he took the cup, saying, 'This cup is the new covenant in my blood; do this, whenever you drink it, in remembrance of me' " (1 Corinthians 11:23-25).

Jesus initiated the breaking of bread that Thursday night, and he told his disciples to continue breaking bread and sharing wine in remembrance of him. And they did. We see this with Hannah and the others in our case study. In fact, they were *devoted* to breaking bread together. But why were they devoted to it? And what difference did it make for them in their new life?

THE BREAKING OF BREAD IS A REMINDER

When the early Jesus followers participated in what has come to be called the Lord's Supper, they were remembering that Jesus had, literally, given his body for them. Every time they broke off a piece of bread and ate it, they were remembering how he had given his own blood and flesh for them on the cross.

This giving of his flesh and blood was not some vague spiritual metaphor about sacrifice. It had been painfully lived out before the apostles' eyes only hours after their Thursday night meal had ended. Jesus had been brutally tortured. He had been mocked and ridiculed and spat at. And then he had a hasty death sentence carried out against him. The tool of capital punishment of the day: prolonged, public death by being nailed to, and hanging from, a crude wooden cross.

But Jesus did not fight back. He didn't try to sway the kangaroo court. And when a mere whisper from him would have forced the Romans to free him, he remained silent. Much like a lamb being led to the slaughter, he walked into this torture and death willingly. He handed over his body. And it was through this literal sacrifice that he was offering life to his followers.

Jesus had stated at one point, "Very truly I tell you, whoever believes has eternal life. I am the bread of life. Your ancestors ate the manna in the desert, yet they died. But here is the bread that comes down from heaven, which people may eat and not die. I am the living bread that came down from heaven. Whoever eats of this bread will live forever. This bread is my flesh, which I will give for the life of the world" (John 6:47-51).

Jesus offered his flesh to make life possible for the world. And so when the earliest Jesus followers took a loaf and broke off a piece and chewed it up and swallowed it, they were remembering his sacrifice and his suffering. And they were remembering what it accomplished for them. Similar to the Passover meal, this breaking of bread was an act of identification: *I* nailed you to the cross with *my sins;* you gave *me* life by offering your flesh.

And when they drank the wine, they were remembering the new covenant that was made possible because of Jesus' blood. Just as the lamb's blood saved the Jews on the original Passover day, so Jesus' blood made a new, eternal salvation possible. When they drank the wine, the early church celebrated this new covenant, knowing that it had been foretold long ago and that it had been fulfilled in Jesus (see Jeremiah 31:31-34; Hebrews 8).

And our three thousand new Jesus followers devoted themselves to doing all this regularly. They were devoted to remembering their King's sacrifice on the cross and what it meant for them. As Paul described their practice of breaking bread and drinking wine, "Whenever you eat this bread and drink this cup, you proclaim the Lord's death until he comes" (1 Corinthians 11:26).

This regular practice drew their eyes, again and again, back to the cross. They chewed the bread, they drank the wine and they remembered. And so can we. As followers of Jesus, we must remind ourselves of the cross by breaking bread and drinking wine.

As I mentioned earlier, a while after becoming a Christian, I started going to church. And to my surprise, a few of the churches I went to didn't talk much about Jesus. I don't want to go into the gory details here, except to say that while sitting through one of these inexplicably devoid-of-Jesus services, we took the Lord's Supper— breaking bread and drinking wine. And that small amount of bread and wine came to me as a refreshing reminder of Jesus and what he had done.

As one preacher has described this value of breaking bread, "Though the pulpit may have failed, the Lord's Supper has still gone on declaring, proclaiming, preaching the Lord's death."*

In our case study we see Jesus followers who were devoted to remembering on a regular basis. And when we take Communion today, we do the same.

THE BREAKING OF BREAD IS A SACRAMENT

Jesus could have simply said to his followers, "Every now and then make sure you are remembering my death on the cross." And they could have lived out this command by saying to each other from time to time, "Hey, remember Jesus died on a cross so we could have life." But Jesus didn't do that.

Instead Jesus modeled and initiated a physical activity that he wanted his followers to participate in. These types of physical activities—initiated by Jesus and for the purpose of growing our relationships with God—have come to be called "sacraments." And sacraments are physical.

In this case Jesus wanted his disciples to break bread and chew it up and eat it. He wanted them to pass a cup around and drink wine. And this is what they did. It is clear from reading the rest of Acts that Hannah and the

---

*Martin Lloyd-Jones, *The Church and the Last Things,* vol. 3 of *Great Doctrines of the Bible* (Wheaton, Ill.: Crossway, 2003), p. 50.

rest of the three thousand (and the ones who came after them too) would stop their lives on a regular basis to come together, break bread and drink wine.

Jesus knew there was something about these physical elements that would aid their memory. So he commanded them to partake in this quite visceral activity in memory of him. It's a process that involves touch and smell and taste. And the images involved are physical and unmistakable. When we tear off a piece of bread and chew, we are reminded of flesh. When we drink the wine, we think of blood being poured out. It couldn't be more memory jarring than that.

Being physical, this sacrament is . . . well, kind of slow. It would be so quick and efficient to just have someone stand up during a church service and say out loud, "Don't forget the cross everyone. Remember his sacrifice!" Total elapsed time: five seconds. Ten perhaps, if the messenger repeats it a few times. But here Jesus initiated a sacrament, which involves the physical, which takes time to distribute, time to chew, time to swallow. And that time is a gift.

Jesus invites us to take part in something physical and slow. "Don't just mention my cross in passing," Jesus seems to say. "Really chew on it (literally) and take it into you (literally). Take slow time to consider and remember." Our culture isn't much into taking time and reflecting. In fact, Communion is often taken out of church services precisely because of its inefficiency. The leaders of the church want a sixty-minute service, but breaking bread for hundreds of people, getting everyone to a big cup (or getting enough little cups out to everyone) just takes a lot of time. Blows the sixty minutes right out of the water.

And yet Jesus commanded his disciples to do something sacramental, physical, slow. He asked them to feel the truth. To participate in it. To take it in.

I remember the first time I attended a Catholic church. It was jarring (and meaningful) to me to realize that the climax of the service was Communion, not the sermon. It was surprising (and sobering) when the priest slowly held up the bread with arms outstretched toward the congregation and sang with meaning, "This is the body of Jesus, broken for you."

I was struck by the reverence, the hush, the quiet, the calmness of coming up to the front and taking my turn to receive the bread and the wine. The experience reminded me of Jesus' sacrifice at a new, deeper level that I hadn't really slowed down enough to experience before.

There was no cathedral for Hannah to go into, of course. In fact, we know that Hannah and the others were breaking the bread in their own homes (Acts 2:46). But we do know that they, too, were slowing down to take part in the same physical, visceral, inefficient sacrament that we practice today. And in this way they remembered the cross of Jesus.

THE BREAKING OF BREAD IS UNIFYING

It would seem from the details of our case study that Hannah and Abram and the rest always broke bread and took wine with other Christians. From Jesus and the disciples in that upper room on Passover night, to the three thousand who broke bread in each other's homes in Jerusalem, to Paul and the Christians meeting late one night in a house hundreds of miles away up in Troas (see Acts 20), the breaking of bread always seems to have been done with others.

It's one thing to quietly remember at home alone. It's quite another to share in a physical, communal act of remembering Jesus' sacrifice. The sacrament of breaking bread has the same feel as the intimate table fellowship we looked at in the last chapter. In fact, breaking bread to remember Jesus' cross is perhaps the most intimate, meaningful expression of table fellowship that a Christian can experience. In this way breaking bread unifies followers of Jesus.

It's unifying not only because you participate in it with others but also because everywhere there are Jesus followers that are doing the same thing. When Paul is breaking bread on a boat in the Mediterranean Sea, Peter is breaking bread in Jerusalem. While Hebrew-speaking Jews are chewing bread in Israel, Greek-speaking Gentiles are chewing bread in Rome.

As Paul, who traveled hundreds of miles through various countries and cultures, observed, "Because there is one loaf, we, who are many, are one body, for we all partake of the one loaf" (1 Corinthians 10:17). No matter what culture you are in, no matter what language is spoken, no matter what shape the loaf is cooked in, no matter how big or beautiful the cup of wine is, it is the same universal table fellowship that followers of Jesus have with one another.

I'll never forget the first time I broke bread thousands of miles away from my home and my culture. The city was Buenos Aires, Argentina. The setting: a dark old building that a young church was using in the middle of one of Buenos Aires's many slum areas. We sat on rickety chairs; we worshiped to guitar and pan flute; and the sermon (given by one of the brothers sitting in the circle with the rest of us) was political, anti-American and spoken in Castillano—a Spanish dialect with a strong Italian-like accent.

The service left me reeling with that culture-shifting dizziness that we all feel when crossing cultures. But then we came to Communion. A loaf was broken and passed around the circle. Each of us pulled off a hunk of bread. A cup was passed around and we all drank slowly, in turn. And I was at home.

I was at *his* table (my new King's table) and was sharing a meal with my brothers and sisters. And I no longer felt the tensions of crossing cultures. I felt unified with my Castillano-speaking family.

Hannah and Abram and Silas felt that unity too. In fact, this is a table fellowship that transcends time. When we break bread today, we are at the same table as Hannah and Abram. And we're remembering exactly what they remembered: the way Jesus gave his body and his blood so that we might live.

WHAT ABOUT ME?

1. Participate in the breaking of bread.

In the early church there were two parts to the church service. First there was the service of the Word, where the Scriptures were taught. Everyone was welcome to come and listen. And after the teaching there was the service of the table, where all those who had been born anew would break the bread and drink the wine in remembrance of Jesus' sacrifice and victory on the cross.

This breaking of bread was commanded by Jesus and is a gift he wants to give to all his followers. So, as his followers, we should be doing this. We should be in a church that celebrates Communion. And we should join the table with the rest of the church.

Except there might not really be a table. And they might not call it Communion. You see, there are lots of different ways that churches have gone about the breaking of bread and drinking of wine over the years. Whatever your church does, just join right in.

Whether it's called the breaking of bread, the Lord's Supper, Communion or Eucharist, the point is the same: eating bread and drinking wine in remembrance of Jesus. For bread there might be a big loaf you grab a chunk from, small crouton-shaped squares, paper-thin wafers or even crackers. For wine some churches have big cups that everyone drinks from, while others have tiny plastic cups for each person. And you'll usually find wine or grape juice in the cup.

At some churches you just stay right there in your seat and they bring the bread and wine to you. At other churches everyone files up to the front to receive the "elements" (the bread and wine) at the front of the church. Some churches give you time to eat and drink at your own pace. Some have places to kneel and pray afterward. Others want you to dip your bread into the cup so you get bread and wine together (and so people don't share colds with each other!).

But don't get too stressed over the mechanics of it all. At first you'll likely find yourself staring around, trying to figure out how your particular church goes about it. It's fine and natural to stare at first. Just remember that the point is to be able to join in, to do some chewing and drinking and remembering of the cross yourself.

2. Remember the cross.

There's obviously something central about what Jesus

did on the cross. He offered his flesh and poured out his blood as a sacrifice for us. And that sacrifice—and all it bought—is something Jesus wants us to be mindful of (physically and viscerally mindful of) on a regular basis.

As we go about breaking bread and taking wine together, we will become more and more centered on Jesus' sacrifice on the cross. His torture there will occupy our hearts. His victory over death will occupy our minds. And the life we receive from his work on the cross will become the music our souls move to.

We will become drawn to passages that foretold this great work. Passages like this prophecy from Isaiah:

He was pierced for our transgressions,
*   he was crushed for our iniquities;*
the punishment that brought us peace was on him,
*   and by his wounds we are healed.*
We all, like sheep, have gone astray,
*   each of us has turned to our own way;*
and the LORD has laid on him
*   the iniquity of us all.*

He was oppressed and afflicted,
*   yet he did not open his mouth;*
he was led like a lamb to the slaughter,
*   and as a sheep before its shearers is silent,*
*   so he did not open his mouth. (Isaiah 53:5-7)*

If you're wanting to deepen or enrich your understanding of what happened on the cross, you could slowly read through one of the Gospel accounts of what happened there in Jerusalem. You could also read some of Paul's words about Jesus and the cross (for example, the first and second chapters of Colossians), since it was something Paul often spoke and wrote about. I'd also highly recommend checking out John R. W. Stott's *The Cross of Christ* (InterVarsity Press, 2006), which takes a thoughtful look at the significance of what happened on the cross.

As we regularly break bread, we will have our minds and hearts drawn back to the cross. And we need that kind of reminder. There are so many subtle ways we can be tempted to forget. Sure, we'll never truly forget the cross and Jesus' sacrifice there, but there are many ways our eyes can be drawn elsewhere.

I have gone through lengthy seasons when I have focused nearly all my energies into contemplating what it means to follow Jesus in radical ways. I can get so myopically focused on how I could be living that I forget to glance at Jesus on the cross. I can study his teachings with such an eye toward radical discipleship that I stop looking at Jesus himself and the greatest thing he ever did. And that kind of misemphasis gets heavy after a while.

What helps bring my eyes back to Jesus is that weekly, inefficient, slow reminder when my church breaks bread together. As my fingers feel the bread and tear off a hunk, my mind is pulled back to that hill where Jesus' flesh was torn for me. As I chew the bread and swallow it, my heart remembers the torture, the cost he paid. As I drink, my soul gets wrapped more tightly around the truth of my own innocence in the eyes of God, because of how Jesus poured out his blood for me.

I think this must be what Hannah experienced as she regularly broke bread and took wine with the others. She and Abram were people of the cross. And so are we. And as we sit at his table together, we have a small foretaste of that day when he will come again and we will all be at table together in heaven: Peter, Paul, Hannah, Abram, Silas . . . *and me,* sitting at the feast together with Jesus.

THE PRAYERS

whispering together with God

There's much more about the new life of Hannah and Abram and the rest that it would be fascinating to look into. (Read all of Acts sometime and you'll see what I mean.) But there's one more part of their new lives that we must take a closer look at before setting our case study aside. It's the fourth thing we're told they were devoted to, and as we see in the details of their stories, it was something they were incredibly strong toward.

They devoted themselves to the apostles' teaching and to fellowship, to the breaking of bread and to prayer. (Acts 2:42)

Young Silas and his friends, who were Jews, already had a rich introduction to prayer. God had called Jews to be a certain kind of people, and that involved a rich life of prayer. Prayer was, simply, people and God talking with each other. It was central and foundational to the entire story we have in the Bible. God longed for relationship with his people, and his people longed to be in relationship with him. So prayer was God and his people whispering together.

But over time their prayer began to calcify a bit. Religiosity began to creep in, and by the time Jesus (who was also a Jew) was on the scene, people not only prayed with prayer shawls and phylacteries but also they wanted to have the *widest* phylacteries on the block. Not only did they pray together but also they began praying *on street corners* with loud, ornate strings of words meant to impress all who walked by.

So Jesus strongly warned his followers against any "prayer" that was really just a performance for the people around them. He also strongly warned against babbling on in long, impressive words and phrases (Matthew 6:5-8).

Instead Jesus suggested again and again that prayer is simply about talking with your Father. You don't have to yell, he said; he's a Father who hears you no matter where you are (Matthew 6:5-13). Jesus prayed often and talked about prayer often, so it only makes sense that after repenting and being baptized young Silas and his friends would devote themselves to prayer. But what exactly did this life of prayer look like?

PRAYER IS WHISPERING

Silas's devotion to prayer and the details we have about the prayers of the three thousand suggest that they assumed God was right at hand. And that he wanted to talk with them. Kind of like children with their father. They prayed as if they could whisper into God's ear.

Silas didn't need to wear a wide phylactery or pray in a certain place. He and the other earliest Christians just prayed. They prayed constantly while hiding (Acts 1:14), while in the temple with others (Acts 2:42; 3:1) and while in a group of people who were all praying the same words together (Acts 4:24). The leaders of the church were people of prayer (Acts 6:4), and so were those deep in sin (Acts 8:22). We see them praying on a roof (Acts 10:9), at an isolated river (Acts 16:13), at midnight on a prison floor (Acts 16:25) and while kneeling on a beach (Acts 21:5).

In other words, they were people of prayer. They were devoted to prayer—no matter what the situation, no matter where they were. They prayed as if God were at hand wherever they went. It seems they remembered what Jesus had said so plainly about prayer.

But with God being invisible, it can be tempting to allow our assumptions about prayer to get into a twist. We forget about his nearness. We assume he is distant. We start praying more ceremonially. We raise our voices as if he might not hear us if we don't. Long, religious words find their way into our prayers.

This slipping away from whispered prayer is subtle. It's hard to notice it happening until the slipping has already started.

One time I was on the University of Colorado campus waiting for a student in the busy student union. It was springtime—that time of the year when the growing coverings on the trees outside seems to be inversely proportional to the amount of coverings that people wear. And while I was waiting for my friend to arrive, several barely clad women walked right in front of me.

My thoughts were varied and mixed. At first I liked what I saw and started to stare. Then I realized that if I gave in to my lust I would feel guilty the next time I tried to pray. Then I began to ponder why God had put such drives in men and such shapes on women. Then I wondered what harm could come from not guarding my eyes and my thoughts. Then I felt alone in this silent struggle on such a loose campus. And then it hit me.

It hit me. I remembered that God was right there with me. And as this realization flooded over me, I blurted out loud in an audible whisper, "Jesus, did you see what they were wearing? You saw it, didn't you?" And just like that my whole posture shifted as I re-remembered how near he was and how I could whisper with him instead of sitting alone with my thoughts and feelings and urges.

A long conversation between God and me ensued. A conversation about lust and T-shirts and the dignity of women and my eyes and our culture. It was refreshing and surprising. He whispered things to me that afternoon that came as a real shock. But the specifics of that time of talking with God aren't the point. The point is how easily I can lose sight of the nearness of God and the true nature of prayer. And how refreshing it is to remember what Jesus said about prayer and about just being a kid talking with his Father.

From the details we get in our case study, it would seem that Silas and his friends believed what Jesus said about prayer. And that's important for us to take note of.

PRAYER IS LISTENING

As we follow Silas and the others forward through the years, we find out that, not only did they say things to God, but also God said things back. Just in Acts, for example, we're told how God spoke to Paul (Acts 22:17-18), Cornelius (10:30-31), Peter (10:9-16), Philip (8:26), Ananias (9:15-16), whole groups of people at the same time (13:2) and . . . well, you get the picture. God spoke to Silas and his friends.

While hearing from God might sound spectacular, it made sense for these new Jesus followers. Theirs was a relationship, after all. God and them being together, talking. Jesus had promised explicitly that the Holy Spirit would come and dwell in his followers. He called that Spirit an "Advocate"—one who comes alongside—and said that the Spirit would teach them and remind them of what Jesus had said (John 14:26).

Since they had a relationship with God, who had

come alongside them, it makes sense that God would say things to them from time to time. That's what relationships are like.

Of course, we are talking about humans having a relationship with the holy, eternal Creator God, who happens to be invisible, so it's not exactly like every other relationship. In Acts we see some Jesus followers who seem to hear an audible voice from God, some who hear from him in a dream, some who hear a mere whisper with the ears of their souls, some who hear him through the apostles' teaching, some who hear from him as a whole group. This hearing from God happens in plenty of ways, but it is clear in our case study that it does happen.

So when we are whispering together with God, it's not just us saying things, but God might want to whisper something to us as well. This is wonderful news. The only problem is, it involves listening.

And we are not so accustomed to listening these days. We are busy, loud, media-entranced multi-taskers. When I drive my car to work, for example, I am usually listening to the news on NPR or listening to a CD or talking on my cell phone (or a couple of these at the same time!). So silence in my life is already pretty rare. And then a year ago I bought my first MP3 player. Wow! All of a sudden there was *never* a reason to have silence in my life. Which makes listening a bit challenging for me. Like it is for many of us, I imagine.

So if we want to hear God's whispers, we need to re-learn silence. And not just the occasional pristine, perfect silence in nature. That deep wilderness silence (where you can hear your neck rubbing against your collar when you turn your head to look around) is wonderful, but it shouldn't be a prerequisite for listening to God. We need to learn how to listen and be quiet even in the midst of our busy days. We don't see Silas and his friends praying only when they go away on a retreat in the mountains or at the beach. We see them praying in the midst of their lives. They made space to listen to their Father.

For me this has meant a conscious effort to not turn on *Morning Edition* on NPR *every morning* while in the shower. Every few days I'll drive without the radio on. I choose a time to walk to the store rather than drive my car. Every now and then I will just sit on my porch (without a book or magazine on my lap even) after my kids have gone to bed and before I turn on the TV. In these small ways I try to draw a line around a pocket of time and create a bit of silence and a chance to listen.

I've found that being silent can be hard, even for ten minutes. It's something we need to grow in and get used to, something we build up stamina for. I've heard some people say that it takes well over an hour for the average person to really still his or her mind, emotions, ideas. Stillness and quiet can't be rushed, it turns out. They take time. Which tells us a little about the reasons why being *devoted* to prayer (not just interested in it) is so important.

PRAYER IS DIVERSE

It is significant to note that among the early followers of Jesus we do not find just a single way of praying. We don't see everyone praying the same words or in the same way or with the same posture. Silas and the rest asked others to pray for them (Acts 8:24), prayed while in times of great confusion and darkness (9:11) and prayed for others who couldn't be with them and were having difficulties (12:5). They gathered for special prayer meetings (12:12), prayed while dedicating people for ministry (14:23) and prayed for the healing of those who were sick (28:8).

Strolling through the rest of their prayers recorded in Acts, we find a multifaceted image of prayer. There are people praying all alone and people praying in groups. We see prayer happening in calm nature and in noisy cities. There's prayer on a day off and there's prayer in the midst of a trying situation. There's prayer with words, in images, in other languages and in deep silence. There are humble prayers asking for leading from God, and there are bold prayers calling on God to act immediately. We see people praying at meals, and we see people fasting before praying.

This striking diversity of prayers shows us that talking with God is dynamic. It can look a variety of ways and have various manifestations. This shouldn't be surprising, since we are talking about people and God in a relationship. An as in any relationship, sometimes our conversations can be serious or informative or silly or silent.

Our conversations are not all the same. I talk with my mother differently than I talk with my wife, which is quite different from how I talk with my kids. My communication is as varied as my relationships. And from what we see in our case study, it's like that for God too.

Again, when Jesus saw people who tried to pray in a certain way and force their prayers to sound a certain way, he counseled his followers to not be like that. And he added, "When you pray, go into your room, close the door and pray to your Father, who is unseen" (Matthew 6:6).

While it is important to get away by yourself (literally) from time to time to pray, Jesus was not implying that we always need to be alone to pray. He, himself, prayed with and around others, and so did his followers. So his point to his disciples wasn't just purely geographic. I think he was also encouraging them to *be themselves* with God. To not try to act differently or try to posture themselves in some way but rather to go into "their room" (into the center of who they are) and there pray to an audience of one: their Father.

In your prayers you have an audience of one as well. It's you and God, eye to eye. Talking about whatever the two of you need to talk about. In the way that only the two of you talk with each other.

Not only is our relationship with God *unique* (he relates with us as an individual), but also it grows and changes as time goes on. There are various seasons of life when our prayer will start to look different or feel different.

I remember how freeing it was for me to realize that I didn't have to pray sitting down for the rest of my life. I had always assumed that prayer was done while sitting, with your eyes closed, with your hands folded. And so that's how I prayed. Then, in my sophomore year of college, an older Christian named Larry asked me if I could pray with him. I told him I could, and so he came by my dorm room and we went outside and started walking. I assumed we were walking back to his place or to a nearby church to pray, but all of a sudden he started talking to God as we walked along.

I didn't know what to do. I peeked over at his face and, sure enough, his eyes were still open. His eyes were open! He was just walking alongside me, talking with God. I glanced around at the other students we were passing on the sidewalk that cut through campus and couldn't believe what we were doing. We were praying while walking. After a while he grew silent and I gathered up the gumption to try it myself. I said things to God right there while walking.

That experience taught me what the Jesus followers

in the early church apparently realized: prayer is diverse. Since then I have prayed out loud while hiking, washing dishes and (my favorite) playing basketball. Maybe those three thousand in our case study never prayed while playing basketball, but their diverse and multifaceted prayers are a testimony to their belief in what Jesus had taught so clearly about prayer—that it's intimate and personal, like kids and their dad talking.

WHAT ABOUT ME?

1. Devote yourself to prayer.

Being a Christian is all about being in a new, dynamic, surprising, intimate relationship with God. Jesus makes this relationship possible. And so being attentive to whispering together with him makes sense. We should be devoted to it. And enjoy it. Not too much else should be said other than that.

Sometimes this will mean praying all alone. Praying alone can look a variety of ways, of course. Some people speak out loud to God; others write to him in a journal; others "speak" silently in their minds; some sing songs to him; some draw pictures or paint as a way to speak with God. People whisper together with him while sitting, while kneeling at their bedside, while standing, while walking. The point is to just be with him. Be yourself. Don't feel pressure to make something happen or force an experience. Just relax. And enjoy whatever the time of prayer brings: silence, words, feelings, conviction, questions, intimacy, boredom . . .

At other times you'll be praying with other people. Followers of Jesus love talking to God together, whether at a church meeting or a small-group meeting or a specific prayer meeting or even just before eating a meal together. Get two or more Christians together and, just like those three thousand in Jerusalem, you'll often find them whispering to God together.

If praying with others is a new experience for you, it might be as shocking and as weird and, ultimately, as freeing as my first time praying while walking with Larry. Be open to experiencing something new. And always remember to just be yourself, talking with God. Don't feel that you have to address God in the same way that the guy sitting next to you addresses him. If it helps you to kneel, kneel—even if no one else is doing it. If it helps you to have your eyes closed, close 'em. If you want to stand, go on and stand.

As you pray in groups, just remember not to get caught up with how you are praying or what you are "supposed" to be doing with your hands or your eyes. Be with God and talk with him as his child.

What matters most is regularly making time for this. That's the posture of devotion we've been looking at throughout these pages. Jesus taught his followers explicitly that they should always pray and not give up. He

As you grow in prayer, you might find the book *Prayer: Finding the Heart's True Home* by Richard Foster (HarperCollins, 1992) to be a great tool to use along the way. It has been a tremendously helpful and enjoyable book for me.

encouraged persistence in prayer (Luke 18:1-8).

And as you devote yourself to prayer, both individually and with others, you will likely find great surprises and growth along the way. Your relationship with God will grow, your ability to still yourself will increase, your ease in being yourself in a group of people will come more easily. All of this happens slowly over time as you devote yourself to prayer.

2. Pray the Lord's Prayer.

As you go along in your devotion toward prayer, you will likely find a great comfort and help in the Lord's Prayer.

Jesus' followers were curious about how Jesus thought they should pray (Luke 11:1). And Jesus did teach them much about prayer. We've already looked at several of these earlier in this chapter, but there are many others as well (for example, Luke 11:5-13; 18:9-14). But one time Jesus gave his followers a model prayer of sorts.

This, then, is how you should pray:
    "Our Father in heaven,
    hallowed be your name,

your kingdom come,
your will be done
   on earth as it is in heaven.
Give us today our daily bread.
And forgive us our debts,
   as we also have forgiven our debtors.
And lead us not into temptation,
   but deliver us from the evil one." (Matthew 6:9-13)

I grew up hearing this prayer all the time. I'd usually say it from memory and not give it much thought. But all this changed for me one summer when I was living in East Palo Alto, California. I was spending the summer after I graduated from college helping to run a summer tutoring program. I was working nearly non-stop, and so when I got an actual day off, I did what I always did when tired: I went to find some books to lose myself in.

Now, it happened that on that day the local library was having its annual book sale, unloading books that were either too damaged or too irrelevant to be checked out anymore. I felt energy enter back into my tired limbs as I browsed through the stacks of cheap books. I started when I noticed a thin volume by Louis Evely. I had read another book by this European priest and so snatched up the book, bought it and went back to my house to lose myself in its musty pages.

The book was titled *We Dare to Say Our Father* (Herder & Herder, 1965) and was about the Lord's Prayer. Once I glanced at the table of contents, I realized this was going to be an interesting book. There was a chapter titled "Our" and another titled "Father" and another called "Who Art in Heaven" . . . and I'm sure you can guess the titles of the rest of the chapters! As I read this book, I began to look at the famous Lord's Prayer with new eyes.

I began to see each of its phrases not as words to be memorized and quickly mumbled from time to time but rather as sturdy vessels to be filled with my own prayers. I began saying the word "Father" not as a simple address to the Lord's Prayer, but rather I stopped after saying it to imagine a Father, to acknowledge my own status as his son, to think of the love and truth a father has for his children. And then, only after filling up this one word with my own prayers, would I go on to the next part of the prayer.

When I prayed the words "and forgive us our debts," I would pause, stopping to confess my own sins. I would lay them all out before God. In this way I was walking slowly through the prayer Jesus had given his disciples. I can *say* the Lord's Prayer in about seven seconds. But sometimes it takes me a whole hour to *pray* it.

Ever since Jesus taught this simple prayer to his followers, it has been prayed again and again in numerous languages and numerous lands by nearly every one of his followers. And that prayer is a gift.

This prayer has been an immense gift to me when my own confusion and lack of words have seemed a block in my prayers. It has given me a place to start. And it walks me through many of the subjects God wants us to be talking to each other about.

And you know what? Silas and his friends undoubtedly prayed through this exact same prayer themselves. It was a gift that enriched their life of prayer as well. The Lord's Prayer was a part of their devotion to prayer, and it can be a part of ours today. Luckily, most of us have the thing memorized already. All that remains is to pray it.

THE REST OF THE STORY

(a conclusion)

Well, you've done it. You've gone and read another book.

In this little book we've followed the events of that day in Jerusalem pretty closely. And following the stories of Abram, Silas, Timon and the others has given us a front-row seat to see the wonder of their rebirth and the joy of their new lives.

But the story was really just getting started that day. The wonder and the joy were just beginning. Read on in Acts and you'll see. No one could have guessed what they were going to do, how they would change on the inside or what they were going to live to see happen.

No one, that is, except Jesus.

SURPRISING, COSTLY AND WORTH IT

Jesus knew, for example, that following him would be surprising, that there would always be new growth among his followers.

When we read on in Acts, we see this surprising

growth. We see waiters becoming martyrs, fishermen becoming preachers, wealthy benefactors becoming vital leaders, persecutors becoming missionaries. Paul, once so vicious and violent, becomes a person marked by joy. Peter, once so callous and aggressive, becomes a person marked by compassion.

Jesus had always taught that his kingdom was like this. "Night and day, whether he sleeps or gets up, the seed sprouts and grows, though he does not know how. All by itself the soil produces grain—first the stalk, then the head, then the full kernel in the head" (Mark 4:27-28). My kingdom is like this, Jesus said. It's about growth.

What kind of growth? Surprising growth. Jesus said his kingdom was like the tiniest of seeds being planted and growing into the largest of trees (Mark 4:30-32). In other words, get ready to be surprised.

Jesus also knew that following him would be costly.

Read on in Acts and you'll see that Abram and Hannah and the rest didn't get to "enjoy the favor of all the people" for long. Soon a deep persecution against Jesus' followers broke out. Repenting and believing began to be costly. Very costly. Most would be mocked and ridiculed. Many would be tortured and killed.

Jesus had always said that it would be that way, that following him would be tremendously costly. "If the world hates you, keep in mind that it hated me first. If you belonged to the world, it would love you as its own. As it is, you do not belong to the world, but I have chosen you out of the world. That is why the world hates you. Remember what I told you: 'Servants are not greater than their master.' If they persecuted me, they will persecute you also" (John 15:18-20).

Following Jesus is surprising. And it's costly. And in the end it's worth it.

Read on in Acts and you get the impression that following Jesus is unquestionably, joyfully worth it. When Peter is arrested for telling the Jesus story, he doesn't hesitate or slow down—he asks God to give him even more boldness (Acts 4:29). When Stephen is being stoned to death for being a Christian, he doesn't abandon Jesus—he remains steadfastly devoted to the apostles' teaching and prayer right up until he breathes his last breath (Acts 7). When Abram, Hannah and the rest have to flee from Jerusalem, they don't pause to lament their new status as refugees—they keep following Jesus and telling other people about him wherever they go (Acts 8:1). When Paul is stoned and dragged out of a city and left for dead, he doesn't wonder if he'd made the wrong choice in following Jesus—he stands up, brushes himself off and walks right back into the city (Acts 14:19).

It is worth it. Jesus had always said it would be. "The kingdom of heaven is like treasure hidden in a field. When a man found it, he hid it again, and then in his joy went and sold all he had and bought that field" (Matthew 13:44).

It will cost you everything. And is unquestionably, joyfully worth it.

THE REST OF OUR STORIES

I, too, have found this adventure of following Jesus to be surprising, costly and unquestionably worth it. Before following Jesus, I was on a path. I was headed somewhere. And that somewhere was not where I am today. I didn't even know that where I am right now even existed!

If I were a betting man, I would have put money on me becoming a lonely, bitter man. A tortured artist at best, wrapped tightly in a net of self-hatred, slipping down greased slopes of addiction (take your pick of which slopes). My money would have been on a future of illegitimate children (mostly unknown to me), a trail of broken hearts left behind me, a tortured nomadic life. That's where I would have put my money.

But then I became a follower of Jesus. I got my own feet dirty, turning from my old life and calling Jesus my King. I was born anew. And in this new life I have ended up somewhere I never would have guessed.

Who would have guessed I'd end up being a peaceful guy, confident that I am loved intimately by God? Who would have guessed I'd end up with a calm heart? I never would have fathomed (let alone put money on) my having so many wonderful, messy people in my life and at my kitchen table. I never would have believed that I would be happily, joyfully, meaningfully married for ten years, or that I would be a father, or that I would not be addicted to anything. Who would have guessed it?

What I've found, after receiving surprise after surprise from Jesus over the years, is that during my conversion I was born into a new land. A land where Jesus is King and I am forgiven. A land with a different landscape and different colors and different horizons and surprises around every corner. Jesus said it would be like that as one of his followers. Mustard seeds, indeed.

As you enter into the rest of your own story, enter in as a newborn. As a child anxious to find out what's next in this new kingdom you've been born into. There's no telling what you'll grow up to become.

As I write this conclusion, my wife and I are only weeks away from the birth of our third child. Wendy's in that big and beautiful stage again. I often put my hand on her belly and feel the motion inside her. And I can't help but wonder about that little one in there.

I can hardly wait for the day (or night) when Wendy will start screaming again and we'll be ushered into the absolute wonder of birth. In the meantime I sit and think of birth and pray in the words of Ephesians 1:18-19 for you who hold this book:

*I pray that the eyes of your heart may be enlightened
in order that you may know the hope
to which he has called you,
the riches of his glorious inheritance in his people,
and his incomparably great power for us who believe.*

WHAT ABOUT US?

(implications for churches)

In each of the preceding chapters I have posed questions that are most fitting for new Christians and for people in the crowd who are still curious about Jesus. I included these "What about me?" sections at the end of each chapter to help these folks be able to reflect deeply and fruitfully on the content of Acts 2.

But I realize there are others who might read this book for the sake of helping and walking alongside the curious and the convinced. If that describes you, then the great news is that walking slowly through Acts 2 can be deeply helpful for you as well. And while I'm not going to pretend that this book is written specifically for you, I do want to highlight what I feel are some of the most helpful questions you can be asking out of each section in Acts 2.

I'm assuming that not all of these questions will be helpful for everyone. My hope is that you might find at least one question for each chapter that leads to some meaningful, helpful reflection. Consider this your alternate "What about me?" section for each chapter.

CHAPTER 1

The Action: *what happened back then?*

- What's the overall message that the curious get at our church?

- Do we have a healthy balance among the different parts of the story?

- If we are overbalanced in one area, which would it be? (For example, some churches are fantastic at dealing with the apologetics questions that arise but never tell the whole story in a compelling way. Other churches might be strong with the metanarrative, telling the Jesus story in creative, fresh, compelling ways, but never really get around to the Call.)

- Do we embrace the importance of each step toward conversion?

CHAPTER 2

The Noise: *are you guys drunk or what?*

- Are we providing answers to the questions the curious have about us and our faith?

- Are we sure to find out what their questions really are and not just *assume* what they are? (This kind of assuming can lead to spending a lot of time and energy answering questions no one is asking.)

- How can we learn what these questions are, and how do we answer them in a language people can hear?

- Where can a curious person among us ask his or her questions freely?
- Is there a way we could facilitate that question-asking better than we are now?

CHAPTER 3

The Story: *can you just start over at the beginning?*

- Is Jesus central to the story we're telling each week?
- How can we grow in our telling of the story?
- Are we speaking about Jesus "to people"—that is, in a language they can understand? Who *are* our people, after all, and what language and culture mark them?
- How does our preparation for a service or study (hours spent practicing, prepping, coordinating) compare with our prayer for a service or study (hours spent be-seeching God to come and cut people to the heart)?

CHAPTER 4

The Call: *where do I sign up?*

- Is there a place in the life of our church or ministry where people can go to hear, specifically and clearly, what it means to become a follower of Jesus?
- Are we calling people to faith? Are we calling them to specific, clear actions that will bring them into the kingdom of God?
- Are we clear about each of the three elements that

Peter is so clear about: what people need to do, what will happen to them if they do and what God's part in it is? Do we tend to focus on one or two of these? Do we tend to ignore one of them?

- Does our church talk about baptism and offer to baptize people on a regular basis?

CHAPTER 5

The Apostles' Teaching: *playing a two-thousand-year-old game of telephone*

- Examine your teaching (over the last six months, for example) and outline what is being emphasized, what themes are being taught on and what is not. Hold this up against the basic message of the New Testament and see what you can see. Where should we spend some more time over the next year? What should we spend less time talking about?

- Is Jesus central to our teaching on a weekly basis? If not, what steps could we take, what commitments could we make to ensure that he is more and more central to what we are teaching on an ongoing basis?

- Perhaps get together with a group of teachers and ask this question together: How are we tempted to be clever, inventive, original rather than faithfully heralding a message we have received?

- Is there any mechanism in place in our church for providing feedback on teaching, so that the teaching can improve over time? If so, what aspects of the teaching are usually commented on (delivery, content, use of Scripture . . .)?

CHAPTER 6

The Fellowship: *the spirituality of the kitchen table*

- Are we encouraging people toward fellowship? Are we providing structures that make that possible? Are we providing so many structures that it's *not* possible?
- Are we teaching clearly about fellowship?
- Which happens more in our body: temple fellowship (everyone together) or table fellowship (small groups of people getting together in intimate, personal settings)? Ask the table question: are people more often together around folding tables here in our building or around each other's kitchen tables in the home?
- Who do I have table fellowship with? Who do our leaders have table fellowship with?
- How is the health of temple fellowship in our group? How could we grow in fellowship when we are all together?

CHAPTER 7

The Breaking of Bread: *chew on this for a while*

- Do we break bread regularly, as we see in Acts 2?

- Do we ever teach about what Communion is, why we do it and how to participate in it?

- Is the sacrifice of Jesus mentioned and remembered, explicitly, whenever we have Communion?

- For some churches, breaking bread has become much less common because it is inefficient and can come across as overly religious. If you find yourself in that place, spend some time reflecting on these questions: Why did Jesus command that we do this? What do we think the experience of breaking bread was like for the three thousand?

- For some churches, "celebrating" Communion (though that's a stretch of the word *celebrate* at times) can easily become assumed, mechanical, somber and devoid of personal meaning. If you find your church more in that camp, spend some time reflecting on the practice as it is recorded in Acts 2 (glad and sincere hearts, in each other's homes, praising God) and ask this question: How can we fully embrace (and not just assume and practice) this sacrament?

CHAPTER 8

The Prayers: *whispering together with God*

- How would we evaluate the prayer life of our body? Would we describe it as a *devotion:* both a disciplined practice *and* a joyfully embraced activity?

- How would we evaluate the prayerfulness of the leaders of our church?

- When was the last time we offered a Bible study, sermon or class on prayer?

- Is there a wide variety of prayer styles exhibited and celebrated in our group, or is there one main way of prayer (liturgical, loud, in tongues, prophetic) that might come across as the only *right* way for new Christians to pray?

- How could we make space for people to pray as themselves talking to God and to guard against their temptation to pray as a performance?